Church Growth Crisis:
The Decline of Christianity
In America

How the Church Growth Movement Has Led
American Churches into Decline and How to
Reverse the Trend before God Exercises Judgment
on America

By Stephen Parker, MA, MS

Edited by: Jo Perryman

Forever Family Publications

Oklahoma City, OK

ISBN-10: 0982870604

ISBN-13: 978-0982870600

See all of our publications at:

www.ForeverFamilyPublications.com

All Rights Reserved ©2011 Forever Family Publications. First printing 2011. The editorial arrangement, analysis, and professional commentary are subject to this copyright notice. No portion of this book may be copied, retransmitted, reposted, duplicated, or otherwise used without the express written approval of the author, except by reviewers who may quote brief excerpts in connection with a review. United States laws and regulations are public domain and not subject to copyright. Any unauthorized copying, reproduction, translation, or distribution of any part of this material without permission by the author is prohibited and against the law.

Table of Contents

Introduction... 5

Message from the Author 7

Part One

Fulfilling the Great Commission: Churches that Aren't

1 Confronting the Church Growth
   Movement World View 11

2: How Did This Church Growth Mentality
   Become So Universally Accepted? 25

3: The Impact of American Positivism
   on the Church Growth Movement 33

Part Two

Fulfilling the Great Commission: Churches That Do

4: Seeking God's Direction in Redefining
   the Mission of the Church 59

5: The Great Commission is Only Fulfilled When
   Each Member Fulfills His or Her Ministry 79

6: God's Instrument for Growing the Church:
   Spiritual Leadership Gifts ………..…………….. 87

7: God's Instrument for Growing the Church:
   Spiritual 'Followship' Gifts ………………....... 107

Part Three

Fulfilling the Great Commission:

Churches that Won't

8: Churches that Won't: The Inertia Church …………... 127

9: Churches that Won't: The Successful Church ………. 147

10: Churches that Won't: The Bunker Church …………159

Part Four

11: Judgment …………………………………..……. 179

Epilogue ……………………………………….......... 187

Resources …………………………………………... 191

Contact Forever Family ……………………………... 192

Introduction

The church in America is facing an unprecedented crisis. This is not a crisis of worship styles or budgets. It is the crisis of continued existence. Christianity is in major decline in the United States and that is not a trend or a temporary downturn. It is evidence of a major shift toward secularism in America. It also demonstrates an unprecedented turn from the God of the Bible as the one and only God to a multi-cultural view of religion (which is idolatry).

What makes this societal turn from God a crisis is that the church is facilitating it. Churches have abandoned the Great Commission in order to attempt to grow by appealing to the selfishness of a generation that has traded service to God for self-service in the name of God. Like a Trojan Horse, the Church Growth Movement has appeared to be a gift to churches, but its methodologies have only led us into decline and ultimately to defeat from within.

Churches are the only ambassadors of Christ to a lost world. With churches in decline, the nation will continue its plunge into paganism and idolatry, which will only precipitate God's judgment on this increasingly immoral nation. If the church does not return to the vision presented to it by God through His Word, then God will have to show the world, through the downfall of the United States of America, the cost of embracing and then rejecting Him. This book is dedicated to the restoration of true discipleship.

Message from the Author

Contained in the following pages is a personal plea from me to you. Unless you and I help the churches with which we are associated change the direction that we have taken, Jesus will remove his lampstand from our midst. We may continue to worship, but we will then no longer be the church of Christ. Once that happens, the downfall of America is eminent.

The information contained in this book will move you. I know, because this material has been presented to thousands of believers like yourself and the response has been exciting to the point of overwhelming. There is a passion for revival that is smoldering just below the surface of our churches.

Even if you believe every word presented in this book, the decline in churches will continue unless *you* do something with the truths contained here. Many Christians view the decline of Christianity in America in the same way that some witness a major automobile accident with fatalities: it is a horrible thing, but what can you do?

Once you have investigated this crisis facing modern churches as well as the solutions to that crisis, you will find at the back of the book the resources and step-by-step instructions needed for you to be a part of the solution, thus helping in your corner of the nation to bring an end to this crisis before it is too late.

Church Growth Crisis: The Decline of Christianity in America

Part One

Fulfilling the Great Commission:

Churches That Aren't

Chapter 1

Confronting the Church Growth World View

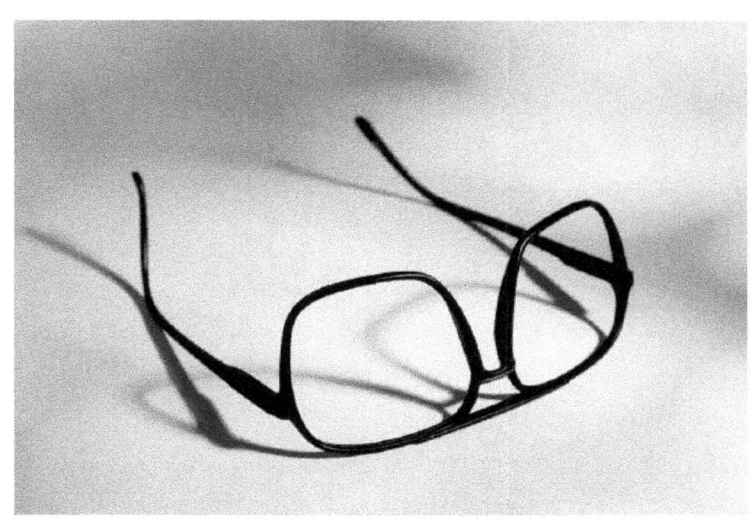

Churches that have followed the direction of the Church Growth Movement are not victims of the current decline in Christianity, but rather they are perpetrators. Granted, such outcomes may not have been their plan or desire, but intentions do not predict outcomes.

The ideologies of the Church Growth Movement are so universally accepted that most church leaders adhere to them without necessarily even being aware that there is such a thing as a Church Growth Movement. It is that monolithic nature of those ideologies that makes reform so difficult. The church growth strategies that have been utilized by the greatest majority of churches over the last few decades have become a world view.

Think of a world view as a set of glasses. The tint on the lenses determines the hue that is observed on everything that is seen. Thus, looking through those lenses one does not see reality but rather the distorted reality presented by filtering lenses. A person described as looking at the world through rose-tinted glasses is understood to be an optimist. Such a one does not see reality. He sees a processed image, a prejudice. He also does not see the negative realities around him because his lenses have filtered those images out. That is what is known as denial. Altering his world view is very difficult because he has continually constructed that way of looking at the world throughout his whole life.

When you direct your attention to the issue of growing the church, whether you realize it or not, you look at the issue from a world view that you have not constructed alone. It has been constructed by your involvement, directly or indirectly, with the thinkers that have emerged from the Church Growth Movement.

Set aside your lenses for a while and try to see the reality that your constructed world view has limited you from seeing. Open your eyes. You might get angry. You might even feel like you have been duped by a conspiracy. There is no conspiracy, at least on the human level. There is just a church growth world view that has become so universal that it is difficult for those within the mind-set to consider any possibilities or strategies except through that mind-set.

It is like the theory of evolution. Among many scientific circles, the world view of evolution is so pervasive, that it is assumed to be axiomatic. Therefore, no amount of evidence to the contrary will be allowed to undermine the belief because the theory of evolution is the lens through which reality is observed.

We emphatically trust our glasses to present a clear picture of reality to the point that we soon forget we are wearing them. Then the images they present are assumed to be reality and therefore not questioned. It is admittedly difficult to look at one's world view objectively because how can a person evaluate his world view except through the lenses of his world view? Glasses without lenses are useless, but the image produced by any set of lenses must be suspect.

If you have accepted, as many church leaders have, that the church must be marketed to lost people in order for it to grow, then you will eventually find yourself in a dilemma. If you offer a ministry or program to touch some "felt need" and the outreach is not successful, then you will feel the need to market harder or differently. You will compete with other churches, which are simultaneously competing with you, to get flashier, bolder, noisier, and in the process, ludicrous.

You find yourself with growing demand on ever decreasing resources (servants). Taken to its extreme, you will become like a church that gives away millions in new cars and other incentives to increase attendance at their Easter service. People come to get door prizes, and the attendance temporarily spikes, but it seems more like an episode from the *Price is Right* than a focus on the Resurrection. If, on the other hand, you are successful in marketing the church, then you will find your attendance grows as the commitment level of each adherent decreases. They came for the services you offered in your advertisements and they are happily lapping them up.

A church built on consumers will eventually be consumed. That is what consumers do. The word consumer literally means to eat or use something up. **Marketing** produces **consumers**. Marketing is a business term that means to sell or to offer for purchase. Throughout time farmers and producers of goods have taken their products to the market place in order to sell them to those that need them. Marketers present their wares for a price, and consumers purchase those goods for a price. Often bartering takes place to negotiate a deal that is acceptable to both parties. However, when the buyer and seller reach an agreed upon price or trade, they consummate the deal and go their separate ways. If there were a ledger, the sheet would then be balanced. That is the end of the deal unless another purchase/barter needs to be made in the future. But how do you keep the consumer coming back to market . . . your *church* market?

Many adherents attend an assembly of the church in search of a deal. They are investing their time, and even a part of their income, although they are not *tithing* or actually *giving* or *contributing* (and certainly not **sacrificing**) because they have been invited to a market. During the age of prosperity, adherents tithed, not as disciples, but with the idea of prospering in return, and "contributions" became a religious investment program promising great returns on money invested. Churches hired an increasing fold of professional ministers to meet the needs of those consumers with the money that adherents were investing while waiting for a return on investment in their personal lives. Eventually the bubble burst. The bubble is based on the economy of the United States, not a great foundation for faith-building.

If church "A" has the best deal, then they will attend there. If church "B" comes out with a better deal, then they will attend church "B." That mentality is what gave rise to the concept of "church shopping."

Modern church-goers do not seek out a congregation where they can best serve, or where they are most needed, or where they can best use their spiritual gifts. They do not attend where the wages of sin are taught and where discipleship to Christ is demanded because that is not a good deal. That is like going to McDonald's as a result of an inviting commercial and then being told by the manager that you must clean up after yourself. That is the old bait-and-switch con.

Marketing churches cannot confront sin, call attendees to repentance, or teach service to one another as an *expectation* of each member. If they do, they know consumers, to whom they have marketed (invited to market to seek the church's wares) will search for a better deal down the road. And it does not matter what the consumers (seekers) are looking for, there is a church that will cater to that desire in exchange for their attendance and the investment of their money for a promised return.

This dumbing-down of sin and discipleship will not only exact at great cost on Judgment Day, it will exact a great cost when such churches can no longer afford to compete with the church that has deeper pockets. And that house of cards will fall as the economy does because market churches depend on the economy. True, disciple-based churches are dependent only on what God does or doesn't do.

Adherents leave assemblies debating whether or not their needs were met. Or they discuss how moving the musical production was or how motivational the sermon was. Was it too long for their liking, or did it have enough stories to keep their attention? Did the preacher use a conversational style or a dramatic style that moved everyone to tears? Did the youth class make Junior want to come back? Were there adequate play areas for little Suzie so that mom and dad could meet up with their friends? Was the church Club-Med enough that the parents could socialize without having to tend to their own children? Would the workers in the youth club deliver the children back to the car so that parents don't have to bother?

There is no end to the possible market-evaluation questions that the young church shoppers can discuss after an assembly. Except what may get lost in that process is that the worship assembly is supposed to be about "kissing the ground toward" God. That is the basic concept of *proskuneo*, the assembly worship word.

Let's get one thing straight, worship is not about you.

Worship is about obedience to, and the glorification of, God. Our English word worship is a contraction of two words: worth + ship. We worship because He is worthy. God has worth-ship so we worship HIM. The fact that you get uplifted from that experience is a byproduct, not a goal.

The message presented in that assembly is not submitted for your gratification. Rather, it is about the preacher fulfilling his duty to God to "preach the Word and be instant in season and out of season." It is also about him fulfilling the following charge from Paul:

> *All scripture is inspired by God and is profitable for* **teaching***, for* **reproof***, for* **correction,** *and for* **training** *in righteousness, that the man of God may be* **complete***, equipped for every good work. I charge you in the present of God and of Christ Jesus who is to judge the living and the dead, and by his appearing, and his kingdom: preach the word, be instant in season and out of season,* **convince***,*

rebuke, *and **exhort**, be unfailing in patience and in teaching. For the time is coming when people will not endure sound teaching, but having itching ears they will accumulate for themselves teachers to suit their own likings, and will turn away from listening to the truth and wander into myths. As for you, always be steady, endure suffering, do the work of an evangelist, fulfill your ministry*. 2 Timothy 3:16-17.

The sermon need only be subjected to one test in order to determine if it is well-pleasing to God: was it true and accurate to scripture? Period! Paul even gives the basis for the test questions with which to for determine the acceptability of each and every sermon. These are the only ones that carry any weight with God:

(1) Did it **teach** ? Did I learn something I did not already know, or was I reminded of something I had forgotten? Teaching means I am confronted with new Biblical truth, or that I am aided in seeing Biblical truth from a new perspective. Teaching and learning are disciplines. Remember that the fundamental concept of *discipline* and *disciple* are the same, and that both words share the same root word.

(2) Was I **reproved?** Reproof is to many a negative concept. We might use the colloquialism "to be called on the carpet." Re-proving is a testing concept that involves one's work being put to the test in order to see if it stands. It is a trial by fire, not a protection of one's feelings.

(3) Did it **correct** my thinking? Correction is the process of taking someone's wrong information

and setting it aright, using scripture. Before someone can be corrected they have to be shown that they are wrong (incorrect in their beliefs). Scripture is useful for that according to Paul. Before someone can be corrected of wrong beliefs or knowledge, she has to seek correction, and thus seek the exposure of her wrong understanding (knowledge) of scripture.

(4) Was I *trained* by the message and its use of scripture? Training is the application of external discipline in the process of growing the person being trained. In football that includes two-a-days in summer heat. In the military, training begins with "basic training" which introduces recruits to muscles they never knew that they had and to endurance of which they never knew they were capable.

(5) Was I *convinced* by this sermon? What I am *convinced* of becomes the basis of my *conviction*. When a sermon convinces, it presents new information in a persuasive way that causes the disciple to leave the encounter with a new conviction. When Peter spoke at Pentecost, Jews who came to a festival thinking everything was okay with God were pierced to the heart to learn that they had murdered Jesus. Those who were convinced by Peter obeyed the gospel to "save themselves from the wicked and perverse generation" (Acts 2:40). Preaching is the most fundamental and profound of all persuasive public speaking.

(6) Was I *rebuked* by the sermon? Have you noticed yet how many of these Pauline descriptions carry a 'negative' connotation? 'Rebuked' simply means scolded. This is what Paul did to Peter, to his face, in the presence of all, when he

was being hypocritical with the Jews and Gentiles at Antioch:

> *When Peter came to Antioch, I opposed him to his face, because he was clearly in the wrong. Before certain men came from James, he used to eat with the Gentiles. But when they arrived, he began to draw back and separate himself from the Gentiles because he was afraid of those who belonged to the circumcision group. The other Jews joined him in his hypocrisy, so that by their hypocrisy even Barnabas was led astray* (Gal 2:11-13; NIV).

Paul opposed Peter! To his face! Because doing right in the sight of God is so much more important than feeling good or not having one's feelings hurt. Leading other people in a proper example is so much more important than one's concern for self-esteem. In fact, self-esteem comes from being right with God. How I *feel* about myself is deceptive.

7. Did this sermon **exhort** me? Exhortation is the next step after a sermon is delivered. The sermon tells people what they are supposed to do in order to obey God. Exhortation motivates them to do it! It usually involves urging or persuading. In the past, sermons were didactic presentations of biblical teachings. They were often followed by a message of exhortation, usually delivered by someone other than the preacher, which urged the congregation to do something with the message they had received. The revivalistic preaching of the 1800's blended sermon and exhortation into the fire-and-brimstone style of preaching that many of us associate with old fashion sermons.

The books written to Timothy are part of a group of Paul's letters that are known as the *Pastoral Epistles*. These are books written by an apostolic preacher to preachers about how to do preaching. Review the words that Paul has used to describe the functions of preaching. Those words form the qualifications of a good sermon: teaching, reproving, correcting, training, convincing, rebuking and exhorting. Are these the words that describe the sermons that you hear or deliver on a weekly basis?

You might find yourself thinking that a modern preacher would not last two months if he preached that way. In other words, people will not endure such preaching. That is why Paul predicted that a time would come when men would not endure sound teaching, but having itching ears they would surround themselves with teachers to suit their own liking (2 Timothy 4:3). Paul warned Timothy to preach the truth in the ways that he described in order to *prevent* apostasy. If you believe that such preaching would not be tolerated today, then we are in the throes of just that apostasy that Paul anticipated. The church cannot grow when it has fallen into apostasy.

The marketing church will attract adherents any way that it can, offering more and more attractions and expecting less and less involvement by the adherents (to avoid the bait-and-switch). Every once in a while they will compare the current assembly attendance with a figure from the past to see if the church is "growing." If such a congregation offers millions of dollars in incentives for Easter, and experiences a 10% increase in attendance on that day, then they can report 'growth.' If they are going to be more credible, and if they are able over the next several weeks to retain 10% of that 10% Easter increase, then they can boast that they have 'grown.' Thus if a congregation of 5,000 sees an Easter attendance of 5500 due to the door prizes that it offers, then it can boast of a 500 (10%) person increase. If three months later they have been able to retain 50 of those 500 new Easter attendees, they can more conservatively boast of a 50 member (1%) growth. Either way it sounds impressive until you remember that the church has not grown at all. It has added consumers (or adherents, not disciples).

A family that invites neighbor kids over for dinner and for free use of the pool has not grown at all. There are more people at the house, more food consumed, and greater need for cleaning the pool, but although there is greater attendance at family functions, the family has not grown. This is playing tricks with numbers. Or more to the point, this is playing games with the concept of church membership. This is exactly where the term "adherent" came from. Adherent is not a Biblical term. Disciple is. An adherent has been defined as a person who attends the services of a congregation but who never identifies himself as a member of the congregation. To some churches, attendance is membership. But roosting in a hen house does not make one a member of the chicken club.

The personal morality of the disciple is dumbed down. The service to fellow members (are adherents members?) of the church is dumbed down. Giving as sacrifice is dumbed down. Spirituality is traded for emotional experientialism in which the effect of an assembly is supposed to approach the effect of a Hollywood-produced drama.

Chapter 2

How Did This Church Growth Mentality Become Universally Accepted?

Every congregation has been influenced to some degree by the Church Growth Movement. Some have followed its philosophies to the extreme and some churches have set themselves against those philosophies. Either way, they are responding to its influence. So what is the Church Growth Movement and how can so many people be influenced by it when many do not even know what it is?

Donald McGavran is considered the father of the Church Growth Movement. McGavran was a missionary in India in the middle of the last century. He observed that the gospel was readily accepted in some geographic locations and that it was either ignored or rejected in others. McGavran coined the term *receptivity* as a way to measure the positive or negative response of any certain people to the gospel. McGavran recommended that missionaries be sent to places of high receptivity and that geographic locations of low receptivity be put at the bottom of the list of mission targets. He even recommended pulling missionaries from areas of low receptivity in order to relocate them to areas of higher receptivity.

McGavran is the first missionary who is credited with the notion that sociological studies could be used to test for receptivity before the expensive enterprise of sending a missionary is undertaken. His efforts represent the beginning of the union of science and mission outreach.

McGavran's work also marked a shift from mission as simple obedience to God to pragmatism (and its associated scientific innovation) as the basis of determining how best to fulfill the Great Commission using human creativity.

The parable of the sower is a biblical metaphor for evangelism. The lead character (an evangelist) cast seed (gospel) everywhere without concern for where it fell. He did not prejudge soil or test for it receptivity. He merely cast the seed wherever he walked. The germination of the seed is determined solely by the interaction of the seed and the soil. The sower threw the seed on the path, with little concern for whether or not it would penetrate. The sower's commission was to sow the seed not to pre-judge the soil. Pragmatism would suggest sowing the seed where it would germinate and take root. God said throw it everywhere. Pragmatism won out. Pragmatism then determined the limits to which God would be obeyed. Pragmatism displaced God as sole determiner of human action in the church. It was a subtle, unplanned, yet profound shift.

The Church Growth Movement is not an organization or an association of churches or ministers. It is a mind-set or a world view. It is an almost universally agreed upon way of looking at the mission of the church. In like manner Political Correctness is not the product of an organization, government, or university. It is a grassroots, agreed-upon way of looking at the political arena. The ideologies of early Church Growth thinkers have been melded into a loosely defined, subjective set of lenses through which to approach the mission of the modern church: ~~making disciples~~ attracting adherents.

Many churches saw their greatest period of growth in the 1960's and 1970's. The post WWII prosperity caused many people to search for a moral and spiritual mooring that would give their lives grounding, direction and purpose. The rise of the Jesus movement as demonstrated in movies such as *Godspell* and *Jesus Christ Superstar* reflected a spiritual renewal among young people. Those volatile times also witnessed the beginning of the rejection of mainstream religious denominations as being traditional, stalwart, and oppressive to the new style of spirituality.

A drive-in church in California grew in popularity because it allowed folks to worship with their families in casual attire, in the comfort of their own cars. Store-front churches began to pop up in the most unusual places as many people seemed to be saying, "Give us Jesus but not the (traditional) church."

The decade of the 1980's saw unprecedented economic growth in the United States. Mainline Christian denominations began a very serious decline in membership. That decade witnessed a greater shift away from the "In God We Trust" national motto to an increasingly secular culture than did any other decade. Americans, for the first time since the nation's founding, began to undertake serious investigation into Eastern and other foreign religions. Meanwhile, leaders in mainline denominations began to panic about their growing loss of membership. It was at that same time that the burgeoning scientific approach to growing the church known as the Church Growth Movement reached its adolescence.

Church leaders turned to sociologists (scientists who study groups of people), pollsters (scientists who report what people are thinking,), marketers (scientists who describe how to present a product to the market), and advertisers (scientists who tell us how to get the message of a product's availability and merits out to the marketplace). By implication, the completion of the mission of the church must require direction by sociologists, pollsters, marketers, and advertisers!

This decade represents one of the most critical junctures in the history of the church in America. Church leaders assumed that they were doing everything right (in accordance with scripture) but that it just wasn't working. American churches had run into a receptivity problem in their own back yards. Church growth pollsters took poll after poll in order to present to church leaders what these emerging young non-church goers were thinking.

Marketers offered advice on how to market the church to a growing segment of people who felt that churches were too mired in tradition to be relevant. If church leaders felt that they were doing what God wanted them to do, and that it wasn't working, that then is a pragmatic problem. Pragmatism is all about what WORKS! And Americans are pragmatic to a fault.

What was missed in this process of retooling for a modern marketplace was the opportunity for restoration. Church leaders should not have assumed that they were doing what is right as a foregone conclusion. They should have taken the rejection of the way that they were doing church as a recommendation that they should seriously reconsider how they were doing what they were doing in light of Scripture.

As we shall see in the second part of this book, God has given us a guarantee that if we will follow what he has called us to do, without turning to the left or the right, that *He will grow his church*. God does not need for us to be innovative, but instead, to be obedient to what *He* has called us to do. It was at this historic juncture that church leaders, influenced by the growing church growth philosophies, decided that God needed their help to grow His church. They turned to human philosophies (sciences) that promised them pragmatic results.

Twenty years later Christianity is in decline in the United States, but since modern churches look at the role of the church through Church Growth Movement lenses, they cannot see that the cause of the decline is the very lenses church leaders use to address the decline. Finding fault with culture is merely blaming the victim.

During the 1990's evangelism and discipleship were replaced by Church Growth ideologies. This was made evident to me from a personal experience that few others have had the opportunity to witness. I moved from the Bible Belt to the Northwest to plant a church during this time. For almost a decade my wife and I started and nurtured a fledgling church, almost in a vacuum. In a very secular part of the country, news from the south was limited. When I had left, authors were writing books about outreach and evangelism, and how to make lost sinners into willing-to-die disciples of Christ. A trip to the local Christian bookstore revealed whole shelves devoted to evangelism. A decade later, when we returned from deepest, darkest Washington, I was shocked to see almost no books on evangelism. Rather, the shelves formerly dedicated to evangelism were now filled with books about how to grow the church. The focus of these two types of books sounds similar, but as we shall see, they are worlds apart.

It is this focal shift away from fulfilling the Great Commission through evangelism toward a focus on how to grow the Church through human enterprise that has lead the modern church into decline. Unless there is a fundamental and pervasive focal shift back to making disciples rather than adherents, the church will fall deeper into apostasy, *leading* the whole society into a downfall of epic proportions.

Either take off your church growth lenses and face the reality of how your obedience to God's word has been impaired by the lenses you have used to interpret it, or remain a part of the problem, rather than a part of the solution. If you choose the latter, you will remain a part of the Christian movement that is leading followers farther away from simple obedience to God, to their own destruction. Are you prepared to give an account to God for your role in that?

Chapter 3

The Impact of American Positivism on the Church Growth Movement

No cultural event or series of events occurs in a vacuum. Darwin was not the only scientist postulating about the origin of species. The Beatles, in any other time in world history, would not have risen to such fame or may not have even existed. The growing discovery of the horrors that Nazi Germany had perpetrated in the war, the post-war poverty in England, and the shock of Kennedy being assassinated in America created a stage that begged for diversion entertainment.

The rise of the Church Growth Movement's ideologies, and the seeming inability of its disciples to objectively look at the results of that ideological influence, has almost been assured by the culture out of which the movement grew. The Industrial Revolution shifted the United States from an essentially agrarian society to a mechanized, manufacturing powerhouse. Folks not born of nobility or of kingly heritage could live out, or dream of living out, the Horatio Alger story of rags to riches. Many of the world's richest men grew out of obscurity and poverty in this social experiment in private ownership and freedom that the world had never seen before.

By the "roaring twenties," prosperity was perceived to be an achievable goal by a greater percentage of the population than ever before. Even the Depression resulted in a generalized mentality of hard work, productivity, and a will to win in order to dig out of the economic hole. World War II mechanized the country even more and opened the work place to women in a greater way.

By the 1950's polio had been almost eradicated and penicillin was being called a miracle drug. There was a general belief that science and medicine would eventually solve every human problem. The buy-in to that idea that science would create utopia was painfully clear when the AIDS epidemic took hold, and Americans *demonstrated* for a cure. Demonstrators believed that putting pressure on the government would result in a cure with money being the only obstacle. In other words, if Washington would only allocate enough money, AIDS would be cured by scientists who can cure anything if they just have enough funding.

The evolutionary idea that everything gets better through the survival-of-the-fittest process added to the American sense that things will get better if we just work hard, creating a uniquely American rose-tinted set of lenses known as positivism. "The Sun Will Come Out Tomorrow" and "Happy Days Are Here Again" could well have been the theme songs for the century of the 1900's in the United States. We still demand that our movies have happy endings and for problems that are presented in our television shows to be resolved in thirty minutes or an hour.

We are the culture that created the ubiquitous smiley face. You can even insert one in your emails so that your reader can "see" your smile ☺! We are the society that presents a glass with water in it and asks, "Is the glass half empty or half full?" Have you noticed that the metaphor of the glass containing water is often utilized to try to convince the half-empty people that they need to be half-full people? If the glass with water represents reality, then there are two perspectives of persons who *project their agendas* on the glass. The optimist looks at the water *and wants to see it being filled*. The pessimist looks at the glass and *wants to see it being emptied*.

The glass is merely a Rorschach test to reveal which kind of lenses you use to alter reality. If the glass is half full, then you use rose colored lenses. If the glass is half empty, you use gray lenses. Optimism is a defense technique that uses denial to ignore the real pain and suffering in the world in order to prevent the Horatio Alger myth from being threatened. Pessimism is a defense technique that uses denial to ignore the joy and happiness in life in order to protect one's self from getting hurt. The glass is neither half empty nor half full. It contains six ounces of water. All other discussion is merely a self-deluding projection agenda. Similar self-deluding projection agendas are **causing** the decline of Christianity in the United States.

In the middle of the last century, when everything in America was booming: industry, education, prosperity, science, medicine, knowledge, business, et al, it was easy to fall into the evolutionary belief that everything would continue to get better. In America, everything grows and gets bigger. As General George Patton said, "Americans love a winner, and will not tolerate a loser." Share-holders expect, not hope for, but expect, an ever-increasing return on their investments. The fans of every NFL team expect their team to win the Super Bowl, and they expect heads to roll if they don't. In schools everyone wins so that no one feels bad about their failure to achieve. This American positivism has led to a mentality that denies failure, loss, or decline. Since such realities do not fit into the agenda that everything is getting better, they are simply denied through rose-colored glasses.

The denial of reality, whether through optimism or pessimism, is a set-up for disillusionment. In fact disillusionment is necessary in order for the optimist or the pessimist to get real. Disillusionment is not having your world crash. Dis-illussionment is witnessing the crash of your illusion. But your illusion needs to crash in order for you to see reality for what it is, good and bad, and to not be injured by its painful aspects.

The illusions of optimism and pessimism are designed to prevent pain by denial of reality. If it is not out there (denial), it cannot hurt me (optimism), or if I believe everything will be bad (denial), I will not be hurt when it turns out to be bad and thus I live with no hope (pessimism). The goal is to see reality for what it is and not be hurt because you expect it to be something it is not (illusion). Denial is the most sought after coping mechanism in America when confronted with something that is potentially painful. The only way reality can break through illusions is through disillusionment.

In the church, American positivism blended with the evolutionary notion that, as Paul McCartney wrote, "It's getting' better all the time," has led to a broken church growth system that we refuse to evaluate in terms of real success, a success not measured by size, but by obedience to God. When the Church Growth Movement ideologies are the lenses that church leaders use to look at the problem of growing the church, they can only see the problem and solutions from within the world view of Church Growth. So if a Church Growth strategy does not work, then it needs to be traded in for another Church Growth strategy.

If "attractional" churches "grew" in the last decade, then that proves that they were successful. An attractional church is a marketing church that uses attractions to get people to their assemblies. The fact that attractional churches are now plateaued or in decline does not disprove the Church Growth logic or strategies, it just means that they need to be traded for newer strategies. How many "attractional" churches are trying to change horses midstream and become "missional" churches? The larger the attractional church, the more painful and costly the adaptation. Yet "missional" is just another fad, more pragmatic innovation. It's merely the Next Big Thing.

Megachurches that were attractional raised a generation of adherents (consumers). How do they then try to now make disciples or "missionaries" (givers) out of consumers (takers)? The church in this view is not universal and timeless, but dependent on, and thus responsive to, culture. Culture, not God, pays the piper and thus calls the tune. When the church gets its focus from culture (which is pagan), then church becomes culture-driven, leading to the most monstrous of all syncretisms: pagan Christianity! That is exactly where we are, but our church growth lenses prevent us from seeing it and recoiling in horror.

If truth is discovered that opposes the theory of evolution, then the evolutionist seeks an explanation for the incompatibility, no matter how wild or convoluted, or he merely denies or belittles the opposing truth. He still believes in evolution because those are the lenses he bought through which to look at the world. The intellectually honest person will look at the newly discovered truth and either reject the theory in its presence, or he will decide to at least investigate the theory further in light of the new information.

When Jews witnessed Jesus performing a miracle (objective proof of his inspiration) some of them rejected their Judaistic traditions and self-definitions (I am a Jew and follow the law, that is who I am) and followed him. By far, and this is very important, the greatest number of Jewish leaders *rejected* him because what he did (like raise Lazarus from the dead) they denied because their lenses filtered out such information. So they decided to kill him and Lazarus too.

The readers who will find it hardest to accept what is written here are church leaders. Those who have invested so much in the Church Growth ideologies will find it next to impossible to reject them in the presence of failure, because rather than looking through Bible lenses, they are looking through Church Growth lenses. They do not know they are wearing lenses. The second part of this book calls for a step-by-step restoration of God's design for how the church grows universally, among all people, with no fads, gimmicks, smoke, or mirrors.

These sincere, well-meaning men and women do not often admit to themselves or to each other the constant fear and pressures they live with. They deny to themselves the continued compromises that they make for the sake of "church growth." They do not share the fear of being trumped by a church down the street with the next explosive church growth gimmick, which will cause them to lose adherents. They don't share or face the pressure that comes with trying to make everyone happy so that no one will leave the church. And they do not share with anyone the guilt that they feel when they study the word of God and are convicted by the sacred trust to reprove, correct, rebuke, and exhort the flock, which they cannot do because adherents have itching ears and don't like those things.

They stick to the illusion that God will accept their work because there are hundreds or thousands of people who said amen. When Paul spoke at Ephesus, he stood in the shadow of the great temple of Artemis (Diana). This was the temple that was reputed to have thousands of temple "virgins," and sex was part of one's worship, to insure that there would be a good harvest. By the standards of justification used by the Church Growth Movement, that church was validated by its size.

I am not a prophet or a son of a prophet, but someone is going to figure out that if you preach to people in the church that they can have sex with whoever they want, and make your argument even marginally palatable, then that church will grow. Churches are using almost everything else pagan in order to grow the church: lotteries, stand-up comedians, rock music, automobile giveaways, beer at the fellowships, pet worship services, ad nauseum. Read that last sentence again. Hello! What have we become? What is truly absurd is when we are in the midst of absurdity and we cannot see how absurd that absurdity is.

Have you ever put the wrong key in your car or front door lock? The key will slide into the lock, but it will not twist to release the tumblers. What do you do when you are convinced that it is the right key? Admit it. Okay I will. I try it again. Then again. Then I take the key out of the lock and look at it, as if I have some kind of locksmith heat-ray vision that can reshape the key. Then I put the same key back in the lock and try it again, as if by sheer will I can force the key to work! In the process, up until this point, I do not even consider that the key is not working because it is the wrong key. The problem was not that my twisting technique was wrong, or that I was not holding my mouth just right. The problem was not that this type of key only works on the third try. The problem was the solution (wrong key) that I was using to solve the problem (locked door).

Unless your church growth methodology can be falsified (it doesn't work because it is wrong) then you will keep trying to unlock church growth issues with the wrong keys. Unless you are open to the fact that the whole church growth problem is not the strategies that we use, but where we get our strategies, then you will keep going back to the Wrong Key Store for a new key to try. You have been convinced that the Wrong Key Store (Church Growth Movement) has the right key (church growth strategy) if you will just try enough of them.

Tent meetings gave way to revivals, which gave way to bus ministries, which gave way to dynamic personas (until a series of them were convicted of crimes), which gave way to attraction, which is giving way to "missional," and on and on and on. We have accepted that fads are necessary. We have accepted that like Disneyland and Six Flags we must keep adding more exciting rides and attractions or the crowds will not come. STOP THE INSANITY. None of it has anything to do with what God commanded, which he has *promised* will be successful.

The most Biblically definitive demonstration that the mainline Church Growth ideologies and methodologies are not from God can be viewed in the lives of the prophets. Many of the men and women that you respect the most were those who spoke the revealed word of God, clearly, and with no editing, to God's people. Many people view prophets as fortune tellers who looked into the future. Very little of what the prophets wrote or spoke about was predictions of the future. The Greek word "prophetes" means forth-teller, not fore-teller. Prophets spoke the words of God that were revealed to them. And they did exactly what Paul charged Timothy (and indirectly every preacher and teacher) to do. And they got killed for it.

Stephen asked the Jewish counsel which of the prophets their forefathers had not killed, implying all of them! God warned Ezekiel that the people he was going to preach to were rebellious. God told Ezekiel that they may or may not listen to him. He also warned Ezekiel not to let the people rub off on him so that he would not become rebellious like they were. Jeremiah was thrown into a cistern for telling people what God wanted them to know. These men were preaching to God's people, not to the lost pagans.

Amos was chosen by God to speak the truth to God's people, even though he was not a prophet. The prophets of Israel had gotten so corrupt that God had to search outside the profession of "prophets" in order to find someone who would tell *His people* the truth. As Amos himself stated, *I was neither a prophet nor a prophet's son, but I was a shepherd, and I also took care of sycamore-fig trees* (Amos 7:14). Ezekiel was a Church Growth failure! Jeremiah was a Church Growth failure! Not only did they not generate a following, they were persecuted at every turn. But they did exactly what God told them to do. They were truth-telling, prophetic, obedient successes, but Church Growth failures. That should tell us something right there.

The most fundamental problems with the Church Growth Movement are its name, its descriptor, and its vision. Its gurus, whom you can find well represented at Christian bookstores, focus on how to grow the church. They use human wisdom to establish strategies for church growth. But growing the church is not the business of humans. God never commanded, asked, or even hinted at the fact that he wants us to grow His church. Once you accept this truth and its implications, you will have discovered one of the most liberating truths that will set you free to minister without worrying about what happens with numbers because God takes care of that. Paul wrote:

I planted the seed, Apollos watered it, but God made it grow (1 Corinthians 3:6).

Our ministry is limited to planting and watering. Paul said so. God is the one who makes the church grow. Jesus said it in his own words:

> *And I tell you that you are Peter, and on this rock I will build my church, and the gates of Hades will not overcome it. I will give you the keys of the kingdom of heaven; whatever you bind on earth will be bound in heaven, and whatever you loose on earth will be loosed in heaven* (Matthew 16:18-19).

Jesus prophesied that HE would build HIS church upon the confession that Peter and others would make, that Jesus was the Christ. We confess . . . He grows. It may just be the height of human arrogance to believe that humans can build the church of Christ. God did not call us to grow the church because we do not have the wherewithal to accomplish it and because we get our goals mixed up when we try to focus on growing the church rather than sowing seed (truth).

The Church Growth Movement has evolved into a pragmatic, innovative think tank. What began as an attempt to united science and mission has resulted in a competitive enterprise that is based on the Next Big Thing. The Next Big Thing is the newest innovation that is purported to give one church the edge over other churches who are striving to increase their market share in the world seekers marketplace. Ironically, much of this attempt at innovation depends on the continued purchase of ever-changing technology. Thus church marketers fell prey to technology marketers.

PowerPoint, utilized through video projectors and large projection screens, promised to make the assembly a visual experience, an innovation that would release worship from a merely auditory stimulus, thus giving the innovative church a marketing edge with an increasingly visual culture. Soon, however, most churches had acquired the technology, at significant cost, and thus the playing field was once again leveled.

Stories abound of the expenses that churches have incurred in order to remain on the cutting edge of state of the art. One church spent a quarter of a million dollars on a sound system that would allow it to create any kind of production for use in their worship assemblies. Interestingly enough, these leaders went to Las Vegas in order to investigate such an amazing sound system. Shouldn't some kind of warning alarm sound when the church is learning from Las Vegas anything at all about how to do church? Oh the blindness wrought by Church Growth lenses.

Just like nuclear proliferation, in which one nation builds more nukes because the other nation has built more nukes, churches have spent amazing sums of money in order to escalate the cold war of Church Growth competitive marketing. Skye Jethani wrote an insightful article in *Leadership* magazine in which he likened this church growth competitiveness to the challenge that Disneyland faces in trying to keep Tomorrowland relevant. When Walt Disney built Disneyland, he added a section of the park that was called Tomorrowland, in which he pictured life in the future. Those kinds of attractions have always been popular at

World's Fairs, for they presented the latest technology plus dreams about an ever-improving, positivistic life in the future. Keeping ahead of technology was an easier task in the 1950's than it is now, with whole technologies that look promising at inception actually faltering by the time they are released due to the emergence of the next technology that will replace them.

Jethani described how Disney was spending millions continually trying to keep Tomorrowland current, and it was breaking the bank. Disney finally decided to go retro, and presented the future from the perspective of the 1950's. That way they could lock the future in time. And save a lot of money. Church growth competitive marketing escalation has gotten to the point, as had Disney, in which the mere outlay of money for technology, buildings, etc., could not be maintained much less justified.

There is no need to get on a soapbox here and speak of all the money that could have been expended on human need rather than on human entertainment, even though there is no evidence that the contribution of the first century church went anywhere else than directly to the needs of people. Rather, what needs to be considered in light of scripture is the acceptability of the foundation of all of this competitive human innovation. God does not need innovators, he needs obedient restorationists.

Moses was a great leader, not because of his creativity, but because he obeyed God to the extent of his strength. In fact, the only disobedience recorded about Moses was when God told him to speak to the rock, and he struck it instead.

Moses took God's command, filtered it with his own mind, and made a substitution that he thought would be just as good, or better, and it cost him the Promised Land. Don't miss the metaphor here.

You have been entreated to remove your Church Growth lenses. Remember that the Church Growth movement began as an attempt to unite science and mission. Science is our word for what we learn from information transferred to our brains from our five senses. There are two types of knowledge in the world: (1) knowledge that God left us to discover (best ways to raise crops, how to cure colic, how to harness energy from oil, etc.), and (2) knowledge that we can only gain through revelation from God (the Bible). These truths are compatible with one another because all reality and all things capable of being known were created by God.

Science and religion cannot be juxtaposed because God created them all. However, since human senses alter the perception of the reality they attempt to observe, they cannot be fully trusted. That is in part why the "facts" of yesterday are replaced with newly discovered or more correctly observed "facts" of today. Many of the "facts" that we believe today will be replaced tomorrow. As a result of the advances in science in the last century, most Americans have a greater faith in humanistic science than is warranted.

In scripture, God treats human knowledge (which includes Church Growth innovation) as suspect. Actually, he views it as foolishness.

> *For Christ did not send me to baptize, but to preach the gospel, not in cleverness of speech, that the cross of Christ should not be made void. For the word of the cross is to those who are perishing foolishness, but to us who are being saved it is the power of God. For it is written, "I will destroy the wisdom of the wise, And the cleverness of the clever I will set aside." Where is the wise man? Where is the scribe? Where is the debater of this age?* **Has not God made foolish the wisdom of the world**? *For since in the wisdom of God the world through its wisdom did not come to know God, God was well-pleased through the foolishness of the message preached to save those who believe. For indeed Jews ask for signs, and Greeks search for wisdom; but we preach Christ crucified, to Jews a stumbling block, and to Gentiles foolishness, but to those who are the called, both Jews and Greeks, Christ the power of God and the wisdom of God.* **Because the foolishness of God is wiser than men, and the weakness of God is stronger than men** (1 Corinthians 1:17-25).

Frankly, we know too much. We depend too much on our own intellect to guide us. Throughout history men have been trying to improve on God's plans and designs. How arrogant we are when we think that God needs our innovation to help him do his job. Have you ever worked in an endeavor alongside someone who was like your right hand? Someone, with whom while working together you almost didn't even need to speak, because that person did the right thing at the right time as if psychic?

On the other hand, have you ever worked alongside someone who was out-thinking you? Someone who was trying to anticipate your next move, but who had no understanding of how you think or your vision for the project? That person was just trying to help, but frustrated you at every step. The person who frustrates you is a person who has not taken the time to learn how you think. Rather, they substitute the way they think it should be done and then expect you to see their wisdom. It is a control issue. That person doesn't listen or learn. That person already knows how to do things correctly. That person needs to be in control. It makes teamwork difficult.

When we try to help God by out-thinking God, we frustrate him and his goals. We will never have the mind of God so we will never be able to anticipate his ways or stay a step ahead of him. We are the apprentices who do not understand how everything will come together, but who, as good workers, obey exactly what the boss tells us to do, only to be amazed when we discover with the completed project that he knew what he was doing all along.

Saul was commanded by God to utterly destroy the Amalekites: *Now go and strike Amalek and utterly destroy all that he has, and do not spare him; but put to death both man and woman, child and infant, ox and sheep, camel and donkey'* (1 Samuel 15:3). Saul's justification for not killing all of the animals is that he was going to sacrifice them to the Lord. No matter what his motive was, God decreed that the kingdom would be taken from Saul because of his insubordination.

> *And Samuel said, "Has the LORD as much delight in **burnt offerings** and **sacrifices** as in obeying the voice of the LORD? Behold, to obey is better than sacrifice, and to heed than the fat of rams. For rebellion is as the sin of divination, and insubordination is as iniquity and idolatry. Because you have rejected the word of the LORD, he has also rejected you from being king"* (1 Samuel 15:22-23).

Don't miss the metaphor here. Worship (offerings and sacrifices) can never trump or replace obedience to God. Even if his motive for out-thinking God was pure and innocent, Saul was guilty of disobedience. Obedience is more important to God than sacrifice. No matter what our gifts are to God, or the motives in our heart for giving them, they can never be acceptable if they are procured in disobedience or in neglect of his direction.

I want to make a plea directly to you. Please do everything within your power to make a difference, to turn this ship around wherever you are using whatever influence you have. If you are a church leader, please take off your Church Growth glasses and reconsider the course you have taken. Please do not get defensive. If this is the first time that you have been confronted with the information in this book, please do not dismiss it. If it is incorrect, or at odds with the teachings of scripture, then by all means reject it.

Not long ago I spoke at a conference for church leaders. There were about 250 church leaders present. For about an hour I made the same plea to them in my presentation that I am making to you in this book. However, due to the time limitations, I was not able to share with them the nuts and bolts of how to change the direction in which we are headed, as I will with you. I merely sounded the alarm and suggested that there was an alternative. I offered access to tools. As I left the podium, I was shocked to find that the message, presented from the Bible, received a standing ovation. I was embarrassed, in part because I was the fourth of four speakers, and none of their messages received such a response.

After the benediction, men came up to me in tears thanking me for the message. And then they went home. There was no follow-up. Like the Greek philosophers we tend to think that if we have learned something new that we are thereby different. However, nothing has changed if we do not DO something different. Those men went home mentally massaged, but they returned to the same routine. Please make a change in your worldview, and then help those around you remove their glasses as well. It is not too late.

If you have been guilty of being a consumer or a pew-warmer in the past, please put this book into the hands of the leaders of your church and share with them from the heart what this knowledge means to you. They will listen to your pleas. And they may, because you have shown passion, give this matter an objective hearing.

You will find that I have either broken or will break many of the rules of writing. I am not trying to be a bad writer. I just find that sometimes the rules, as good as they may be, do not fit the given situation. One of the rules of writing religious literature is to not quote a lot of scripture. That rule is a response to the style of the old days when much writing was merely scriptures tied together with a little commentary. It was a time in which a sermon was considered a good one if it contained thirty or forty scripture quotations. Why not just read scripture instead of preaching? It is a fine line.

If I am going to make an impassioned plea against the wisdom of men, and for having a "thus sayeth the Lord" for everything we do, how can I do so without offering "thus sayeth the Lord" statements? Since I hope you would not trust my paraphrase, please accept the following quotations from God himself. Please do not glance over them, even the familiar ones. Read them afresh with your Church Growth lenses removed, and consider: is the fear of God before your eyes? Truly?

> *Trust in the LORD with all your heart, and do not lean on your own understanding* (Proverbs 3:5).
>
> *See to it that no one takes you captive through philosophy and empty deception, according to the tradition of men, according to the elementary principles of the world, rather than according to Christ. For in Him all the fullness of Deity dwells in bodily form, and in Him you have been made complete, and He is the head over all rule and authority* (Colossians 2:8-11).
>
> *And you neglected all my counsel, and did not want my reproof; I will even laugh at your calamity; I will mock when your dread comes, when your dread comes like a*

storm, and your calamity comes on like a whirlwind, when distress and anguish come on you. "Then they will call on me, but I will not answer; they will seek me diligently, but they shall not find me, because they hated knowledge, and did not choose the fear of the LORD. They would not accept my counsel, they spurned all my reproof (Proverbs 1:25-30).

Counsel is mine and sound wisdom; I am understanding, power is mine. By me kings reign, and rulers decree justice. By me princes rule, and nobles, all who judge rightly. I love those who love me; and those who diligently seek me will find me (Proverbs 8:14-17).

Woe to those who are wise in their own eyes, and clever in their own sight (Isaiah 5:21)!

"Woe to the rebellious children," declares the LORD, "Who execute a plan, but not Mine, and make an alliance, but not of My Spirit, in order to add sin to sin; who proceed down to Egypt, without consulting Me, to take refuge in the safety of Pharaoh, and to seek shelter in the shadow of Egypt! Therefore the safety of Pharaoh will be your shame, and the shelter in the shadow of Egypt, your humiliation" (Isaiah 30:1-3).

Who has directed the Spirit of the LORD, or as His counselor has informed Him? With whom did He consult and who gave Him understanding? And who taught Him in the path of justice and taught Him knowledge, and informed Him of the way of understanding (Isaiah 40:13-14)?

"Who is this that darkens counsel by words without knowledge? Now gird up your loins like a man, and I will ask you, and you instruct Me! Where were you when I laid the foundation of the earth? Tell Me, if you have understanding, who set its measurements, since you know? Or who stretched the line on it? On what were its bases sunk? Or who laid its cornerstone, when the morning stars sang together, and all the sons of God shouted for joy (Job 38:2-7)?

The conclusion, when all has been heard, is: fear God and keep His commandments, because this applies to every person. For God will bring every act to judgment, everything which is hidden, whether it is good or evil (Ecclesiastes 12:13-14).

"There is no fear of God before their eyes" (Romans 3:18).

The completeness of scripture to do what God needs done:

All Scripture is inspired by God and profitable for teaching, for reproof, for correction, for training in righteousness; that the man of God may be adequate, equipped for every good work (2 Timothy 3:16-17).

. . . seeing that His divine power has granted to us everything pertaining to life and godliness, through the true knowledge of Him who called us by His own glory and excellence (2 Peter 1:2-4).

Is Your Congregation using Church Growth Methodologies to Attempt to Grow?

1. Does any part of your outreach strategy involve inviting (attracting) people to worship assemblies?
2. Do you advertise the church on television, in yellow pages, on billboards, or through other media?
3. Do you order your worship assemblies to meet the desires of visitors?
4. Do you use terms like "seekers," "adherents," or "unchurched" rather than "lost?"
5. Is sin confronted in sermons and classes?
6. Are your outreach methodologies adding servant-disciples to the church, who then minister to others?
7. Is the size of your attendance the measure of your faithfulness?

Church Growth Crisis:
The Decline of Christianity in America

Part Two

Fulfilling the Great Commission:
Churches That Do

Chapter 4

Seeking God's Direction In Redefining the Mission Of the Church

The Great Commission

16 But the eleven disciples proceeded to Galilee, to the mountain which Jesus had designated. 17 And when they saw Him, they worshiped Him; but some were doubtful. 18 And Jesus came up and spoke to them, saying, "All authority has been given to me in heaven and on earth. 19 "Go therefore and make disciples of all the nations, baptizing them in the name of the Father and the Son and the Holy Spirit, 20 teaching them to observe all that I commanded you; and lo, I am with you always, even to the end of the age."

Matthew 28:16-20

'Job One' of the Church

The Great Commission is comprised of three parts:

1) Make disciples.

2) Baptize them.

3) Teach them to observe all things that I have commanded you.

The Great Commission is Authoritative

The Great Commission is 'job one' of the church. It was given with a formal declaration of its importance, probably so that we would not underestimate its significance. Jesus had directed his apostles to assemble on a mountain in Galilee once his ministry had been completed at the cross. It is telling that even at that point some of the eleven still doubted. They had seen all that Jesus had done, and had witnessed the results of the resurrection and the appearances of the Christ, and some still doubted. Total trust in Christ and total obedience to his words is so difficult for human beings. We should not be surprised that two thousand years later we have to battle with our own trust and obedience, even those who are professed church leaders.

Jesus preempted the Commission with a statement of authority: "**all authority has been given to me in heaven and on earth.**" Officials give authoritative statement when they are passing on a responsibility of grave importance. At the end of a wedding ceremony, a minister might say something similar to, "by the authority vested in me by the state of Texas, and as a minister of the gospel of Jesus Christ, I now pronounce you husband and wife." It matters little that the couple is starry-eyed and not paying attention to a word that he says at that point, rather waiting to hear the words, "you may now kiss the bride." The words are still authoritative and binding. They mean that when Preacher Jim pronounces them husband and wife, he does so by the authority of the state. He is acting as an agent of the state and he has bound them together legally as an official of the state.

No one, who has not been authorized by the state, can stand before a couple and legally bind them together. They have no authority to do so. If anyone other than an official certified by the state stood before the couple and pronounced them husband and wife, that person would have violated the law, and the marriage would be null and void. The pronouncement is more than just words.

In a message to preachers (via Timothy), Paul makes a similar authoritative statement that should give every preacher pause:

> **I solemnly charge you in the presence of God and of Christ Jesus, who is to judge the living and the dead, and by His appearing and His kingdom**: *preach the word; be ready in season and out of season; reprove, rebuke, exhort, with great patience and instruction. For the time will come when they will not endure sound doctrine; but wanting to have their ears tickled, they will accumulate for themselves teachers in accordance to their own desires; and will turn away their ears from*

the truth, and will turn aside to myths (2 Timothy 4:1-4).

I solemnly charge you. Paul has mustered up his most serious frame of mind and wanted Timothy to know that. When Jesus said "verily, verily," or "truly, truly," he was emphasizing that what he was saying was important. If we say, "listen to me," or "hear this," we are emphasizing the importance of what we are saying. Paul gave Timothy (and indirectly all preachers) a charge. A charge is

> **1a:** the quantity that an apparatus is intended to receive and fitted to hold **b:** the quantity of explosive used in a single discharge **c :** a store or accumulation of impelling force <the deeply emotional charge of the drama> **2a: obligation, requirement b : management, supervision** <has charge of the home office> **c:** the ecclesiastical jurisdiction (as a parish) committed to a clergyman **d:** a person or thing committed to the care of another **3a: instruction, command b:** instruction in points of law given by a court to a jury **4a: expense, cost** <gave the banquet at his own charge> **b:** the **price** demanded for something <no admission charge> **c:** a debit to an account <the purchase was a charge> **d:** the record of a loan (as of a book from a library) **in charge:** having control or custody of something <he is *in charge* of the training program> (Mirriam-Webster's Online Dictionary).

The notion of a charge carries with it several concepts that are worthy of investigation. A charge is something that is given as an obligation, a requirement. It consists of a matter or quantity that is to be received and held.

Since Jesus has all authority in heaven and on earth, no one else has the qualification to give the charge to the church of what it is supposed to do, or how it supposed to do it. That means no pastor, preacher, eldership, church board, church growth gurus, or all of them combined, has the right to augment the mission, purpose, worship, or outreach directions that the church has received from its owner, Jesus.

I had a college professor who used to say, "When you see a 'therefore' you had better investigate what it is there for." Jesus immediately linked his authoritative statement with a 'therefore' that connects his statement of authority with his following commands. Thus he was saying: I have all authority everywhere, THEREFORE, go make disciples of all nations. We are to make disciples of all nations because he commanded us to do so with total authority!

Make disciples
The first part of the great commission contains the imperative to make disciples of all nations. Much has been made of the command to "go," but go is not the imperative in this statement. In fact the "go" is actually a participle. It should literally be translated, "having gone" or "being gone." The going is assumed. In fact the going is happening every time we leave our homes. We are already moving about in the world. The reason the "go" is usually translated as a directive (imperative) is because that seems to be the

only way to get to "all nations." But the word translated nations is *ethne* (from which we get ethnic). The focus is on making disciples of all ethnicities. This is probably a reflection of "to the Jew first and also to the Greek." The focus is not on where the people are (geographic nations) but on the all-inclusivity of all ethnicities of people. The imperative is not to go to them. You are already doing that as you interact with people of all different kinds of ethnicity. The imperative is to make disciples of them.

There is no authority given to create adherents, members, attenders, consumers, or any other classification of people's association with Christ other than as disciples. I am sure that there are remnant churches that are using the gospel only to make disciples only, but it must be admitted by all that they are few and far between. If the pulpit is not consistently calling folks to reject sin and take up their crosses in selfless service to the body of Christ, then the church is not making disciples, regardless of how many people are in the pews, how large the budget is, or how many hours of TV airtime are purchased in the name of Christ Jesus. If the church is not making disciples, it is not obeying job one given to her by the direct, authorized command of Jesus, the church's owner!

Please remember the parable of the vineyard owner and the stewards that he left in charge of his vineyard.

> *"Listen to another parable. There was a landowner who planted a vineyard and put a wall around it and*

dug a wine press in it, and built a tower, and rented it out to vine-growers, and went on a journey. And when the harvest time approached, he sent his slaves to the vine-growers to receive his produce. And the vine-growers took his slaves and beat one, and killed another, and stoned a third. Again he sent another group of slaves larger than the first; and they did the same thing to them. But afterward he sent his son to them, saying, 'They will respect my son.' But when the vine-growers saw the son, they said among themselves, 'This is the heir; come, let us kill him, and seize his inheritance.' And they took him, and threw him out of the vineyard, and killed him. Therefore when the owner of the vineyard comes, what will he do to those vine-growers? They said to Him, He will bring those wretches to a wretched end, and will rent out the vineyard to other vine-growers, who will pay him the proceeds at the proper seasons." Jesus said to them, "Did you never read in the Scriptures, 'The stone which the builders rejected, this became the chief corner stone; This came about from the Lord, and it is marvelous in our eyes'? Therefore I say to you, the kingdom of God will be taken away from you, and be given to a nation producing the fruit of it" (Matthew 21:33-44).

If our unauthorized transition from making disciples to making adherent consumers seeking entertainment is not a usurping of a vineyard that does not belong to us, then how will this parable ever be applied? To be negligent with the most basic responsibility given to us by Jesus, who gave it after claiming authority to do so, is to beg to be treated the same way as the vine-growers. Look at the last sentence of that scripture.

If we continue to fail to obey the Great Commission, given in authority by Christ, then the Kingdom of God will be taken away from its place in America and given to a nation that will obey him. He did so to the rebellious Jews, and he will do so to us. That will happen regardless of whether or not there are groups of people gathering on Sunday morning to give him praise. They may be a religious organization or a worship society, but they will not be the church of Christ, because he is not their head and they are not his disciples. It is the responsibility of church leaders to see to it that disciples are being made!

Disciples are created through the gospel

In Matthew 28, Jesus gave the command to make disciples. In Mark's account of the Great Commission, the how-to of making disciples is defined.

> *And He said to them, "Go into all the world and preach the gospel to all creation. He who has believed and has been baptized shall be saved; but he who has disbelieved shall be condemned"* (Mark 16:14-17).

In this parallel passage, Jesus commanded his disciples to preach the gospel to all creatures. This is the Greek word "euangelion" or "evangelion" from which we get the word evangelism. The word literally means good news. It is by this gospel that people are saved (Romans 1:16). Here is another place that many are confused. If you ask most Christians what the gospel is, they will tell you it is the Bible. It is not. Allow scripture to define the gospel.

> *Now I make known to you, brethren, the gospel which I preached to you, which also you received, in which also you stand, **by which also you are saved**, if you hold fast the word which I preached to you, unless you believed in vain. For I delivered to you as of first importance what I also received, **that Christ died for our sins according to the Scriptures, and that He was buried, and that He was raised on the third day according to the Scriptures*** (1 Corinthians 15:1-5).

The Bible is scripture. All scripture is inspired by God (literally "God-breathed," 2 Timothy 3:16). The Bible, however, is not merely good news. The Bible contains good news and bad news. The earth opening up and swallowing thousands of people is bad news. The descriptions of hell are bad news. The prediction of Jesus coming with flaming fire in vengeance is bad news. The Bible also contains good news, the best of which is the gospel, the "good news." So all scripture is inspired and the scriptures contain the gospel, which is the death, burial, and resurrection of Jesus Christ. So the gospel is a subset of the Bible (scripture). It is the good news subset of the Bible.

Jesus commanded his disciples to make disciples of all the nationalities by preaching the gospel. The church is not to be used as the method of fulfilling the Great Commission. We were not commanded to invite people to church. The use of the church instead of the gospel of Jesus to attempt to fulfill the Great Commission is so universal, that it is not even seen as being unauthorized, not commanded, and thus sinful. "Everyone is doing it" does not make it right. Again, this is where Church Growth glasses have blinded us to obvious truth. Just look at the advertising (marketing) that churches are using to try to grow. Pick up any Yellow Pages directory and turn to the 'churches' sections. Look closer at the church-sponsored billboards as you drive to work. It is all about attraction *to the church*. Such advertisements include a focus on:

1. The worship experience
2. The facilities (magnificent cathedral, state of the art electronics, etc.)
3. The playground for the kids
4. Parking shuttles
5. State of the art nursery
6. Youth group
7. Singles ministry
8. Drama ministry
9. Special classes
10. Other? _____

What church is not using similar methodologies to attract people to church? To church! That is not the command though. Use the gospel (that is the only methodology that Jesus authorized) to make disciples of all people. This investigation into how properly functioning churches grow has not even gotten into biblical meat and already the methodologies espoused by the Church Growth Movement have fallen short of obeying even the first part of the Great Commission. The root concept of "sin" (*harmatia*) is to miss the mark.

Baptize them

The second commandment of the Great Commission is to baptize the people being discipled. Disciples are made with the gospel. Salvation comes through the gospel. The gospel is the message of the death, burial, and resurrection of Jesus. Then how does the gospel result in the command to baptize? It should come as no surprise that there is also confusion about the relationship of the gospel and baptism. Regardless of that confusion, part of the Great Commission, job one of the church, is to baptize believers:

> *"Go therefore and make disciples of all the nations, **baptizing them** in the name of the Father and the Son and the Holy Spirit"* (Matthew 28:19).

The relationship of baptism to the gospel is made even more emphatically by Mark in his account of the Commission:

> And He said to them, "Go into all the world and preach the gospel to all creation. **He who has believed and has been baptized shall be saved**; but he who has disbelieved shall be condemned" (Mark 16:15, 16).

Once a person receives the message of the death, burial, and resurrection, she must do something in order for it to be applied to her. In Mark's account, the initiation of her saved relationship with Christ, because of the gospel, begins once she has believed and been baptized. To express that as an equation, it would read:

$$\text{Belief} + \text{Baptism} = \text{Saved}$$

Or broken down further, it would read:

He who has believed
(past perfect, already accomplished)

$+$

has been baptized
(past perfect, already accomplished)

$=$

shall be saved
(future result)

    Paul demonstrated the relationship between salvation and this baptismal obedience to the gospel in 2 Thessalonians 1:7-9:

> *. . . when the Lord Jesus shall be revealed from heaven with His mighty angels in flaming fire, dealing out*

> *retribution to **those who do not know God and to those who do not obey the gospel of our Lord Jesus**. And these will pay the penalty of eternal destruction, away from the presence of the Lord and from the glory of His power.*

Jesus will return some day in vengeance against two types of people, (1) those that do not know God, and (2) those who do not obey the gospel of Jesus. The response to the gospel is given in the Great Commission: preach the gospel and whoever believes and is baptized will be saved. Churches that do not practice obedience to the gospel will not make the gospel the focal point of their existence. It is easy to understand why they will neglect the use of the gospel and only the gospel as their church growth methodology.

Teach them to observe all that I have commanded you.

The first two parts of the Great Commission deal with how to initiate the discipleship process with someone who is not yet a disciple: preach the gospel to them, and then help them obey that gospel. At that point, according to Mark, they are saved. The beginning of the discipleship relationship with Jesus coincides with the initiation of the saved relationship with Christ, which coincides with obedience to the gospel through belief and baptism. That is what the Great Commission teaches. That is not what most churches teach.

Once salvation has been initiated and the believer's sins are taken away (he is saved) through obedience to the gospel, then a disciple is born.

The third part of the Great Commission instructs that the new disciple must be taught to believe and practice (observe) *everything* that Jesus has commanded. How much is there to teach? Well consider it this way: The first four books of the New Testament are called 'gospels" because they tell us the story of Jesus. The next book, *Acts of the Apostles*, tells how people responded to the gospel and became Christians, thus how the church grew (and thus by example how it grows today). The next 21 books of the New Testament are written to Christians about how to remain faithful to this relationship with Christ. The New Testament then closes with the book of Revelation, the book of prophesy about how the church will prevail.

There is one book in the New Testament that describes how to make disciples and 21 books that describe how to keep the saved saved. The first two parts of the Great Commission (presenting the gospel and helping the believer obey the gospel) can be completed in an hour or two. The third part of the Great Commission will take the rest of his/her life. This is what is often known as follow-up, or, at least initially, New Christians ministry.

It is now time for another self-test. Most modern churches are not making disciples as commanded, but rather attracting worshipping consumers. Most modern churches are not using the gospel of Jesus Christ to grow as commanded, but rather they are attracting people to the church. Are most churches teaching their disciples to obey everything that Jesus has commanded? We need to be brutally honest with one another and hold one another accountable in these matters because we will stand before God one day and give an account for every deed and every word. You hold me accountable and I will hold you accountable. Please!

The truth is that in most churches attractional messages and attractional classes are being taught. Not doctrines (teachings, commands)! From how to get a job, or how to find a spouse, to Christian aerobics and 'stressbusters,' the message has been dumbed down to not offend anyone. **True disciples are never offended by truth!** They seek it, and they want to get to the meat of true spirituality. Honestly, with your Church Growth glasses taken off, how is your congregation doing with any part of the Great Commission? I will bet that folks are not being added to the church daily like they were at Pentecost. If they are not being added to the church daily where you worship, is it because the Great Commission is being fulfilled as commanded and it just isn't working? Are you prepared to tell that to God?

The three parts of the Great Commission involving preaching the gospel (evangelism), baptism, and follow-up (teaching), create and sustain disciples. Evangelism is a part of discipleship. Baptizing is a part of discipleship. Teaching obedient believers everything that Jesus has commanded (doctrines) is a part of discipleship. Many Christians mistakenly think that the Great Commission is about evangelism. Evangelism is only a part. In fact, as we will soon explore, the Great Commission is the umbrella under which every function of the church takes place.

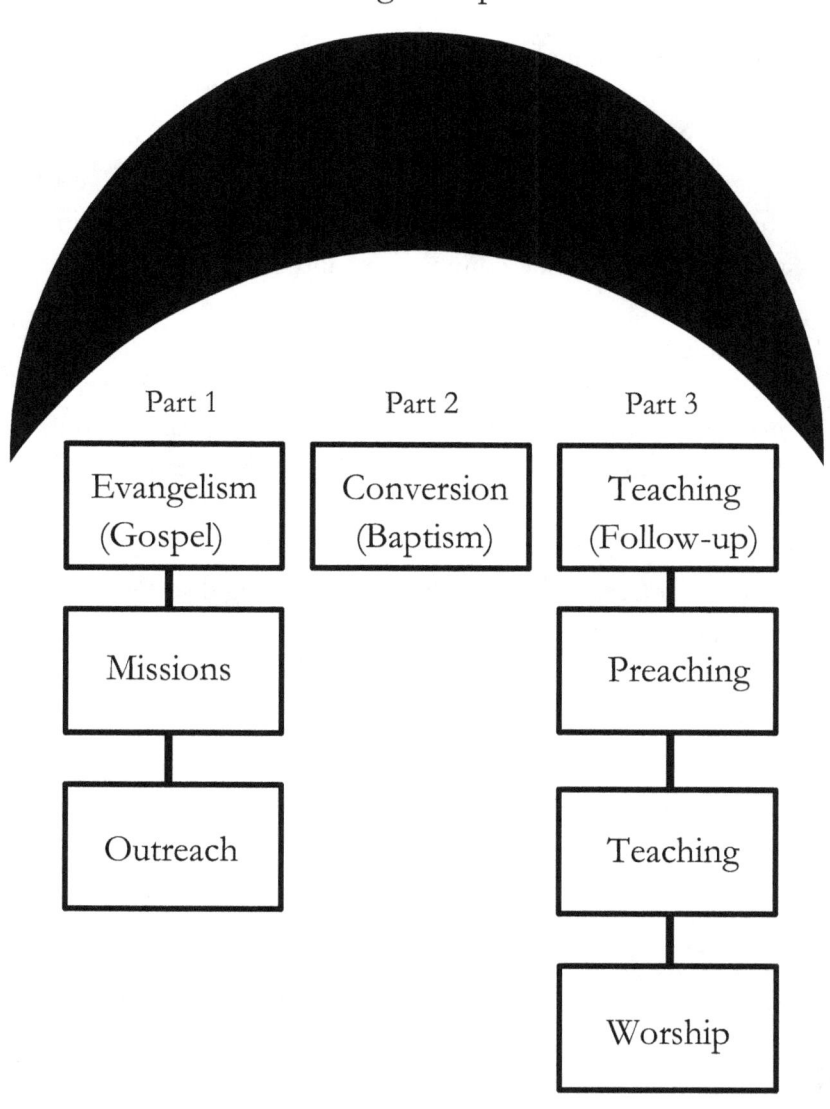

Making and growing disciples is the full function of the church. Taking care of one another is what disciples do as a result of being taught to observe all things (including loving and serving one another). The *motive* for fulfilling the third part of the Great Commission, observing (obeying) all things commanded, is the first part of the gospel, the message of the death, burial, and resurrection of Jesus. We give, sing, pray, love, serve, take communion, and forgive one another, etc., as parts of the commandments we are learning in our growing discipleship (follow-up that never ceases until we die). The gospel is why we do them . . . *we love because he first loved us* (1 John 4:19) . . . *but God demonstrates his own love for us in this: While we were still sinners, Christ died for us* (Romans 5:8).

The Great Commission, making and growing disciples, is the full mission of the church.

Chapter 5

The Great Commission Is Only Fulfilled When Each Member Fulfills His or Her Ministry

If you have passed the self-tests so far, and are feeling ready to stand before God and give account for your stewardship, be warned that we have just begun to explore the how-to's of fulfilling the mission of the church. You will be very hard pressed to find a church that is fulfilling the next biblical teachings. The church is declining for a reason. The culprit is ignorance of, or negligence with, the full teachings of God. We have much work to do! Fortunately, what God has commanded us to do in order that he can grow his church is actually easier and more enjoyable than all the things we are trying to do and at which we are failing.

One of the greatest misunderstandings that has been fostered upon God's people is that everyone is responsible for evangelism. There has been so much damage done to good people, so much guilt borne by so many good-hearted martyrs. The following statement is true and worthy of full acceptance:

Every member of the body is responsible to fulfill his or her part of the *Great Commission*.

Or

Every member of the body is responsible to fulfill his or her part of *making and growing disciples*.

Those statements differ greatly from:

Every member is responsible for evangelism.

As we have noted, evangelism is a subset, a part of the Great Commission. We are beginning to see the damage that results from the fallout of viewing the Great Commission as only about evangelism. Oh, the carnage that has been wrought by well-meaning teachers who have said:

> "No one makes it to heaven alone. Unless you bring another to heaven, you yourself will not make it."

> "This church can double in size in one year if each of us would just bring one to Christ."

> "Everyone in the church is an evangelist. Have you done your part?"

Have you ever sat in the audience as an evangelist filled you with guilt for having never brought another person to Christ? Have you ever walked the aisle in tears to repent of your failure to be an evangelist, while at the same time filled with the dread that you will be no better an evangelist after you have confessed than you are now in repenting? The guilt has driven countless away. The guilt is part of the reason why the church has stepped back from stressing evangelism. It makes Christians feel guilty.

Have you ever been so riddled with guilt about the pressure to share the gospel that when you finally mustered up the courage . . . no the nerve . . . to try to convert someone that it seems more like an ambush? Please allow the following scripture to release you from that guilt and sense of failure.

*And He gave **some** as apostles, and **some** as prophets, and **some as evangelists**, and **some** as pastors and teachers . . .* (Ephesians 4:11-12).

This passage is not presented in order to alleviate your guilt, pain, and suffering, but because what it teaches is true. The fact that it alleviates your guilt, pain, and suffering is merely a byproduct of taking God at his word rather than at the word of others. According to this passage, evangelism is a gift ("he gave . . .") given to *some*, not to all. In fact, in this list of gifted abilities, the recipients of these gifts are differentiated from one another. The idea could also be expressed as: he gave some to be apostles, and others to be prophets, and others to be evangelists, and others to be pastors and teachers (as long as we understand that these gifts are not exclusive of each other. Some people are multi-gifted).

In spite of the fact that the Bible teaches that God gave SOME to be evangelists, many will hold to the traditional teaching that everyone needs to be an evangelist even though the Bible nowhere makes such a statement. That is the power of misunderstanding the Great Commission as being solely about evangelism. That is also the power of tradition. That is also the power of confusing truth from the

Bible with what my favorite preacher(s) or teacher(s) once said. So as long as tradition is worshipped in churches, that bit of madness will continue to be taught, and casualties of good people will be the result. The scripture of God giving the "gift" of evangelism to some does not preclude the other statements about each person's responsibility to the Great Commission:

Every member of the body is responsible to fulfill his or her part of the *Great Commission*.

Or

Every member of the body is responsible to fulfill his or her part of *making and growing disciples*.

Everyone who is not fulfilling the responsibility to make (or initiate) disciples (the role of an evangelist) is responsible to fulfill his or her part in growing disciples that evangelists have initiated. The fuller context of that last scripture will provide the foundation for discovering how such is accomplished. Please pay very close attention to this passage.

> *And He gave some as apostles, and some as prophets, and some as evangelists, and some as pastors and teachers, for the equipping of the saints for the work of service, to the building up of the body of Christ; until we all attain to the unity of the faith, and of the*

knowledge of the Son of God, to a mature man, to the measure of the stature which belongs to the fulness of Christ. As a result, we are no longer to be children, tossed here and there by waves, and carried about by every wind of doctrine, by the trickery of men, by craftiness in deceitful scheming; but speaking the truth in love, we are to grow up in all aspects into Him, who is the head, even Christ, from whom the whole body, being fitted and held together by that which every joint supplies, according to the proper working of each individual part, **causes the growth of the body for the building up of itself in love** (Ephesians 4:10-16).

Chapter 6

Spiritual Gifts:
God's Instrument for Growing the Church

Spiritual Leadership Gifts

God's Blueprint for Growing the Church!

Ephesians 4:10-16

God has not left us with the Great Commission yet with no teaching about how to fulfill it. He has not abandoned us to trial and error. He has not left us to human wisdom. He certainly has not left the most important task in the world up to our innovation. Yet because this information is new to us, a deeper investigation of exactly what it teaches is warranted.

God has gifted certain people in the church with certain abilities in order to lead the flock. These are leadership gifts, and they are described in verse eleven. *God gave (gifted) some to be apostles, some to be prophets, some to be evangelists, some to be pastors and some to be teachers*, in order that the flock has the leadership that it needs to move forward and accomplish what God has given the church to do (the Great Commission). Later the roles of each of those leaders will be investigated more deeply. Together, these leaders have one major function:

. . . for the equipping of the saints for the work of service, to the building up of the body of Christ.

According to this passage, the main function of church leaders is to equip the saints for the work of service. Every Christian is a saint (Colossians 1:12; Romans 1:7; Philippians 4:23; Ephesians 1:1, 3:18). Every Christians is a minister (the Greek word is *diakonias*, servant). In most modern churches, ministry is performed by members of the church "staff." Some denominations call them clergy. The term clergy is used to describe persons who have been ordained by their denomination to be ministers. The term clergy is not a biblical one. Neither is "staff." The concept of ordination of preachers is also not a biblical concept.

When words are created that are not biblical words, confusion is the result. When words are created that are not biblical words and which do not convey even a biblical concept, apostasy is the inherent danger. It is best to stay with biblical words and biblical concepts. Thus we learn from this passage, regardless of what 2000 years of church history has wrought, that the primary function of church leaders is to equip "members" for ministry.

The term equipping (literally down-equipping, adjusting) is a useful word. To equip is to present the equipment necessary to complete a task. There is a task (ministry, service) that is required of each Christian, and it is the responsibility of the these listed leaders to give each of these saints the equipment they need in order to fulfill the service required of them. The context of the passage will destroy three non-biblical concepts: (1) a church board as leaders, (2) adherents or consumers as "members" of the church (saints), and (3) marketing the church as church growth.

Church leaders are to be intimately involved with each and every saint in order to insure that they are equipped for ministry. Leaders are not supposed to replace saints in ministry, as is the case in most modern churches, but rather to prepare each Christian for ministry. The result of that equipping is given in the next phrase of this passage: *to the building up of the body of Christ.* The body of Christ, the church, is built up through the process of equipping members of the body for service. Before we delve deeper into God's church growth methodology, let's take a closer look at who these leaders are.

Apostles

While the term apostle in Greek means "one sent" the New Testament use of the word is limited to the twelve who were chosen by Christ to fulfill the role of giving transitional leadership to the church until a permanent leadership could be developed. The only additions to that number were Matthias who replaced Judas (determined by the casting of lots, a method that was used to allow the Holy Spirit to "call" the replacement) and Paul who was set apart by Jesus at Damascus. The qualification for the role of apostle is given in Acts 1 (he must have been in the presence of Jesus from the beginning till the end of his ministry). This role and its unique qualification have been fulfilled and it is no longer existent on the earth, but it obviously was still extant in Paul's day, at the time of the writing of this epistle.

Prophets

As mentioned earlier in the discussion of what constitutes

biblical preaching, *prophetes* means forth-teller. This is actually the biblical word for preacher. A prophet is one who tells God's people what God wants them to know and to do. Because we are a fallen people living in a fallen world, the majority of that instruction is remedial, or corrective. That is why it often seems painful. Some folk get confused about the role of a prophet because in biblical times prophets received the words of God through direct revelation from God (which they then wrote down for our use). They then shared those words with God's people while being careful not to edit the meaning of the revelation they had received.

Today a preacher or prophet receives the message of God from the scriptures. That is God's revelation "once and for all delivered to the saints." Like the Bereans who Paul honored in his day, you and I can search the scriptures to see if the prophet speaking to us is a true or false prophet. If he tells us what God tells us in scripture, no more, no less, then he is a true prophet. A prophet must reveal the whole council of God to his people.

Evangelists

Evangelists are specialized prophets because their message is the gospel and their hearers are lost people. Evangelists share the gospel of the death, burial, and resurrection of Jesus with lost people and help them to obey the gospel once they have received it. Peter's sermon at Pentecost is a great example of evangelism because he shared the gospel and then shared how to obey the gospel once those with pierced hearts asked him, "Men and brethren what must we do" (Acts 2:37)? Whereas prophets preach the whole counsel of God to his people, evangelists share the gospel with the lost.

Pastors

Pastors are quite simply shepherds. These are the men who watch over and direct the sheep (flock, church). Unfortunately, due to centuries of Roman Catholic influence, the roles of prophet, evangelist and shepherd were combined into a function called "priest." There were no priests presiding in first-century churches. In fact the priesthood (as a human sin-advocate between God and man) was destroyed at the cross. Every Christian is a priest (1 Peter 2:9), and has direct access to God through Christ (the High Priest).

Teachers

Teaching is the bringing forth of information. For teaching to take place, there must be learning. For learning to take place there must be information. Information is difference. The teacher is one who knows something that the student doesn't know, and imparts that information to the unlearned student. The main difference between preaching (*prophetes*) and teaching (*didasko*) is that preaching is motivational. It calls people to change. Teaching calls people to know.

Congregations of the one church are the local groups of saints (priests) who have received the gospel from an evangelist and have been added to the church through that gospel. They are overseen and directed by a group of pastors (shepherds, elders). They receive God's message from prophets (preachers) and are taught the word of God by teachers. All of those leaders work together to make ministers of each of the disciples that are a part of the body of Christ.

Unfortunately, the apostate and biblically incorrect model of the church being presided over by a priest has never been fully eradicated from New Testament churches. Some call him Father, some Pastor, some Preacher, some Padre, some Reverend, some Parson, and many other names. They are all variations of the role of an Old Testament priest. He is the one who runs the church, who presides at worship, who leads the prayer at potlucks, who visits the sick, who teaches the lost, who drives the bus, and who makes repairs at the building. Put him in a robe, a suit, or a sport shirt. Call him Pastor, Father, or Brother with a capital 'B.' It is because of this unbiblical role that churches have leaders that function as corporate boards, and "laity" that does not function at all. This ungodly church structure is part of the reason for the decline in Christianity in America.

Prophets speak forth the word of God. Evangelists share the gospel. Pastors shepherd God's people. Teachers give instruction about the Word of God. When all of these gifted leaders work as a team to equip the saints for works of ministry, there is no limit to what can be achieved by God through his church. That point is made even more powerfully in the last verse in this section of scripture:

. . . from whom the whole body, being fitted and held together by that which every joint supplies, **according to the proper working of each individual part, CAUSES** *the growth of the body for the building up of itself in love* (Ephesians 4:16).

Unity in the church is not maintained by everyone agreeing on everything. Unity is accomplished by Christians working together as a body, as a single unit made up of many parts, who function together like a well-oiled machine in accomplishing God's purpose for the church. The church, according to this passage, is held together by what every "joint supplies."

As a child I was taught that unity would be achieved by all Christians being in agreement in everything. The attempt to get everyone on the same doctrinal/opinion page led to debates that brought about just the opposite outcome: division. The more brethren argued to try to get to agreement, the more division resulted. Maybe that is at least part of the cause of the striation of Christianity into so many denominations, which has occurred since the Renaissance.

That is what is so powerful about this metaphor of a body. Our bodies are made up of so many members that have such a variety of functions, yet they work together in such a uniform way. Together they accomplish what any of the parts alone could never even attempt. So it is with the body of Christ.

God has designed marriage in such a way that opposites attract. Different roles, different world views, and different genders guarantee that they will not always agree on how to address various challenges. But the *bond* of marriage causes them to find a way to work together in spite of their differences.

Members of a football team have different roles, duties, tasks, and even different ways of viewing the game as a whole. What unites these players of such variety of tasks and personalities is working to achieve the same goal. The conflict that they endure among themselves is what insures that the team's goal is achieved, not the goal of any particular player. So it is in the body.

The church is held together by what *every* joint supplies. If any joint fails, then the members attached to it are limited in their ability to function also. If your right elbow fails, it severely limits the function of your right hand, your fingers, your wrist, etc.

Paul emphasized that last point by adding: *according to the proper functioning of each individual part.* This is where professionalized ministry has dramatically impaired the function of the church. Professionalized ministry is what has created the unbiblical concept of members of the body of Christ being an "audience." The clergy/laity divide (neither word is found in scripture) has led to the perception of performers on a stage in worship and an audience of critics who sit in judgment of their performances. The movement of attractional churches toward entertainment in their assemblies is actually a natural progression of this performer/audience mentality that comes as a result of "professionalized" ministry.

Do not confuse "professional" ministry with supported ministry. Don't confuse being supported to perform ministry with being "hired" as a minister. Paul was supported to spread the gospel when people believed in what he was doing and wanted to be partners in his work (Galatians 6:6, Romans 10:14,15). If he had been hired, then he would be a hireling. Scripture takes a dim view of hirelings (John 10:12, 13).

Supporting a minister is merely giving him time. When Paul supported himself, some or much of his time was spent making tents. When Paul was fully supported by the brethren, all of his time was spent in evangelism. There is a trade-off each way. There are advantages and disadvantages with each approach. That is why Paul used both means of support (self-support, support by partners) depending on what was best in any given situation.

Every Christian is a minister. Some are supported and some are self-supported. Scripture teaches that certain ministries require so much time that they necessitate support by others in order to insure that the minister is able to properly fulfill his function. Return to the metaphor of the body. The stomach only works when there is food to digest, otherwise it remains dormant. The heart is never dormant. The body needs both organs, and they cannot be given greater or lesser value, but they function in different ways. One function demands much more time to fulfill than the other. Most people give greater support to their hearts than to their stomachs. They need them both equally, but one organ's time demands brings it greater attention (support).

What causes the church to grow? That is the question that countless church growth gurus and books attempt to answer. The trial of their theories is being attempted in thousands and thousands of churches across the land, with little effect. It is amazing that millions are spent on church growth materials every year, and yet Christianity and the membership and attendance of most churches are in decline.

Like the winner of a lottery or the occasional winner at a casino, the isolated "success" of a few keep the others plowing away at the latest theories but with no success. And those few megachurches that have large numbers of people . . . are they successful from God's perspective? Are they making disciples using the gospel, and equipping every one of them for ministry? Or are they swelling in attendance by attracting consumers to a list of buffets to be consumed?

God said that the church grows according to the proper functioning of each individual part. In fact this passage uses the word "causes." There is a guarantee imbedded in the use of the notion of causality. While Church Growth gurus present theory after theory, and metaphor after metaphor,

Paul speaks about cause and effect. It is a bold statement to say that if one does A then B WILL result. That is especially the case with matters that utilize human involvement.

Linear causality is the notion that there is predictability of outcome that can be controlled by input behavior. If you understand the laws of geometry, and you allow for the friction of the felt when you line up the eight ball between the cue ball and the corner pocket, you can predict where the eight ball will go. I can tell you as a therapist that linear causality does not work with humans. I can suggest an intervention that you might attempt with another person, but I can never, nor can anyone else, predict the response by that other person. That is because that person has a will and a set of emotions of their own. People cannot be forced to respond like billiard balls. Yet through Paul, God boasts of a guaranteed outcome of growth for the church, when and only when each individual member of the body is functioning properly within his/her specific ministry.

There are qualifiers to this linear causality of growth, however. Each member must function and each member must function properly. How many of your physical body parts can you lose before your ability to function as a whole becomes disabled or impaired?

I have never seen my liver, and I hope to never see it. I could not describe it to you and probably could not identify it if it were presented to me. I am totally unsure of exactly what it does or how, but I love my liver and I hope that it will function perfectly up until the time I die in my sleep of natural causes. After all my liver has "live" in its name. Even though I cannot identify my liver or even properly describe its workings, I would be dead without its function. How many dead body parts does it take to choke the life out of an otherwise healthy body?

How many churches are attempting to fulfill their mission with a body that is devastatingly impaired and dysfunctional? How many churches, as they swell, become increasingly dysfunctional because they keep adding body parts that demand nutrition and blood supply but offer no service to the other body parts? Hiring more professional staff members does not address the problem, much less solve it.

Review what we have learned so far:

1. The purpose of church leaders is to equip Christians for ministry (service), not to replace them in ministry.
2. The purpose of equipping members for service is so that the body can be built up.
3. Unity of the body (church) is only achieved through that (ministry) which every Christian minister supplies to the body.

When each individual part of the body is functioning properly the body builds itself up in love. That means that the church is self-perpetuating. Any complex system, like a body, must have energy continually infused into it, or the body will die. Living organisms consume resources in order to produce energy.

In most churches, church leaders must continually infuse the system with new resources in order to provide energy to continually fuel the church. Even a plateaued church consumes a lot of resources in order to merely maintain existence. That is a massive drain on the limited resources that leaders can provide. That is one reason for the high level of burn-out among professional ministers. That is also a reason that so many ministers fall into immorality and other moral problems, to escape from the continual emotional, physical, and spiritual pressure of being a mother bird who must work endlessly to feed the never-ending chirping of baby birds crying for food.

When each member is involved in ministry, the body builds itself up. The nourishment that each member (minister) draws from the head (Christ) provides resources that each member can then *add* to the body. As we will soon see, performing ministry based on one's gifts does not drain one's batteries, but rather recharges them. So each member of the body, rather than being a drain on the body, is a source of new spiritual resources for edifying the body.

The last two words of this section of scripture are the most important in the context, for they are the foundation upon which this body is built: love. Service is love put into action. Jesus made that clear when he washed the disciple's feet:

> *It was just before the Passover Feast. Jesus knew that the time had come for him to leave this world and go to the Father. Having loved his own who were in the world, he now showed them the full extent of his love. The evening meal was being served, and the devil had*

> *already prompted Judas Iscariot, son of Simon, to betray Jesus. Jesus knew that the Father had put all things under his power, and that he had come from God and was returning to God; so he got up from the meal, took off his outer clothing, and wrapped a towel around his waist. After that, he poured water into a basin and began to wash his disciples' feet, drying them with the towel that was wrapped around him* (John 13:1-5, NIV)

Love is not oriented toward self. Consuming is all about self. Service is about finding joy in loving like God does, with an outward focus. Entertainment centers on how I feel about the stimulus that I am being presented. The root of the problem of decline in Christianity in America is selfishness. Churches have tried to cater to an increasingly self-absorbed culture in an attempt to grow the church by becoming codependent to that selfishness.

The ugliest aspect of capitalism is that it caters to the lowest appetites of humanity, vanity, insecurity, greed, etc., in order to sell something. Churches have unwittingly fallen into the same trap. Churches cannot afford to follow the lead of culture, for Christians were called to change culture, not to adapt to it. By catering to the baser motives of mankind, churches are salt without saver. Church leaders should know better because Christians are the only leaven whose service God can use to change the world.

There is no discipleship in calling folks to join a worship society, or even worse, an entertainment society. When culture rebelled that worship to God was boring and old-fashioned, rather than responding to this discipleship dilemma by calling for discipleship (take up your cross), church leaders sought how to change the nature of church worship in order to make it palatable to self-absorbed people. It was not their church or worship to tinker with, for it belongs to Christ and only he has the authority to make its "policies." The problem of church attendance is a discipleship problem, and discipleship is a response to the gospel. The problem of church attendance is a problem of improper response (anything other than love) to an improper invitation (anything other than the gospel).

But how will church leaders who have been trained by tradition to function as either apostles or governing board members retool to become biblical leaders? Once again there are answers found in scripture. But before we turn away from this passage, notice the serendipities that the church receives when it takes God at his word. Not only will the church grow, but many of its most basic problems will be solved in the process. Look at the passage again with the following emphases added:

> *And He gave some as apostles, and some as prophets, and some as evangelists, and some as pastors and teachers, for the equipping of the saints for the work of service, to the building up of the body of Christ;* **until we all attain to the unity of the faith**, *and of the knowledge of the Son of God,* **to a mature man, to the measure of the stature which belongs to the fulness of Christ**. *As a result,* **we are no longer to be children, tossed here and there by waves, and carried about by every wind of doctrine, by the trickery of men, by**

> ***craftiness in deceitful scheming****; but speaking the truth in love,* ***we are to grow up in all aspects into Him, who is the head, even Christ****, from whom the whole body, being fitted and held together by that which every joint supplies, according to the proper working of each individual part, causes the growth of the body for the building up of itself in love* (Ephesians 4:10-16).

On the road to biblical church growth, some of the most basic obstacles facing modern churches will be removed. The first is unity. Unity can never be achieved among consumers because consumerism is based on competition and competition is based solely on the desires of the self. As Charles Colson explained in *Against the Night*:

> *When the not-so-still voice of the self becomes the highest authority, religious belief requires commitment to no authority beyond oneself. Then religious groups become merely communities of autonomous beings yoked together solely by self-interest and emotion.*

The second achievement on the way to church growth is maturity. To attract folks to worship in order to use worship as a magnet to create disciples is a bait and switch con. As an old preacher once stated, "Whatever you use to get them in you will have to use to keep them in." There is nothing that compares with the gospel to not only save people, but to keep them motivated to serve. That is why the gospel is what we are called to use to bring people to Christ (not to the church).

One cannot achieve maturity without the discipline (training) that is the root of being a disciple. Yet no one seeks maturity who is not willing to count the cost for training and stretching. The apostles were called to die. So are we. Growth that comes through equipping members for discipleship service is the only path to maturity. Study after study of the levels of sin in the church demonstrates that there is a mental break between joining a church and living a morally upright life. There is a maturity breakdown that is being enabled by modern religion in its self-centered modern form.

The third serendipity that is discovered on the path to biblical church growth is discernment. Paul promised that as a result of being equipped and involved in ministry we will no longer be like naïve children who will follow anyone who has candy. In order to "grow," churches have so watered down truth and doctrine in order to not offend that there is a crisis of belief. That is an inherent problem in using the church and its assemblies to try to grow the church.

In many churches, there is such paucity of real teaching that the situation has gotten beyond "winds of doctrine" to the need for real discussion on whether or not there is right and wrong teaching. If truth and error cannot be identified, then there can be no such thing as a false teaching or a false teacher. While on one hand everyone likes to be a part of the club that accepts everyone, at some point being a member of a club that anyone can walk into or out of has no meaning, and therefore no respect. Religions that give meaning, purpose, and direction (those are doctrines by the way) will fill the vacuum, as Islam has begun to do. Woe be unto us as Christians if we are creating of Christianity something that is "common and unclean."

The process of equipping members for ministry forces us to properly define goals, direction, doctrines, etc. To equip an evangelist, leaders have to define who is lost and who is saved. Body members have to know which body parts they are connected to, and thus servants of. Body parts don't migrate from one body to another at will. The goals, direction, and mission must find their parameters defined in scripture. It is only when people are equipped that these definitions have to be addressed, and it is then that it is imperative that scripture be utilized for establishing such equipping parameters. An army (another biblical metaphor for the church) is never told, "Go out there and find somebody to fight, and do something negative to them."

Chapter 7

Spiritual Gifts: God's Instrument for Growing the Church

Spiritual 'Followship' Gifts

Once church leaders are convinced that their main ministry is the equipping of the saints for works of service, what then? Most leaders would not even know where to start. That is understandable since this aspect of leadership ministry has gone virtually unrestored for at least as long as any of us have been alive. Once again, God has not left us without resources. Consider the following basic call to discipleship that has been almost totally misunderstood:

> *I urge you therefore, brethren, by the mercies of God, to present your bodies a living and holy sacrifice, acceptable to God, which is your spiritual service of worship.* ***And*** *do not be conformed to this world, but be transformed by the renewing of your mind, that you may prove what the will of God is, that which is good and acceptable and perfect.* ***For*** *through the grace given to me I say to every man among you not to think more highly of himself than he ought to think;* ***but*** *to think so as to have sound judgment, as God has allotted to each a measure of faith.* ***For*** *just as we have many members in one body and all the members do not have the same function, so we, who are many, are one body in Christ, and individually members one of another.* ***And*** *since we have gifts that differ according to the grace given to us, let each exercise them accordingly: if prophecy, according to the proportion of his faith; if service, in his serving; or he who teaches, in his teaching; or he who exhorts, in his exhortation; he who gives, with liberality; he who leads, with diligence; he who shows mercy, with cheerfulness* (Romans 12:1-8).

The first two verses of this chapter have been used out of context in most every church. They are used as the basis for a call to holy living, usually in order to encourage Christians not to use their bodies for worldly things like smoking, drinking, sex, drugs and the like. While that case can be made as application, it really misses the whole point of the context.

Reread the scripture above and as you do, inflect the words that are bold. You will notice that the bold words are conjunctions that join what precedes with what follows. You will then see that the eight verses are one continual thought. Paul explains in verses three through eight **how to** fulfill that challenge of the first two verses.

The passage teaches that each of us has received a spiritual gift or gifts from God, and that our spiritual service of worship is to use that gift or those gifts in service to the body. Presenting your body to God as a living sacrifice does not mean that you do not use drugs. It means that you present the gift(s) that God gave you back to him as a stewardship, and you do so by fulfilling your ministry in the body through service to other body members. That is not only how you present your body as a sacrifice, it is also how you resist being conformed to the world.

You will not become self-absorbed and insensitive to the needs of others, which leads to using people. Rather, through ministry you become increasingly sensitive to the cries around you. To live in Christ means:

> It is not about you. Get over yourself. Serve someone! That is your **DESTINY**.

Then you will prove what the will of God is. The world does not know that it is more blessed to give than to receive. The world does not know that in order to gain your life you must lose it. We have to accept God's teachings that we do not understand and submit to them. That is what a disciple does. Then, we learn through experience that his way really does work. His will is then proved. Faith is rewarded with sight.

Churches today do not believe that making disciples by presenting the gospel will work. They do not believe that the church will grow by leaders equipping disciples for ministry and cutting them loose to minister. They believe that it takes lotteries and car giveaways to build a church. Their fruits betray them. Other self-righteous churches blame the megachurches for selling out doctrine in order to grow, but they themselves are doing little to obey God either. Inactivity is not the solution for mistaken activity.

We will never see biblical, first-century spread-throughout-the-planet type growth until we believe that God will bless our obedience to his commands, even when they don't seem to make sense. Or maybe that is *especially when they don't make sense.* When have God's ways ever made sense to humans, be they disciples or not?

Churches Grow When Christians Use Their Spiritual Gifts in Service to the Body

> *For just as we have many members in one body and all the members do not have the same function, so we, who*

> *are many, are one body in Christ, and individually members one of another. And since we have gifts that differ according to the grace given to us, let each exercise them accordingly: if prophecy, according to the proportion of his faith; if service, in his serving; or he who teaches, in his teaching; or he who exhorts, in his exhortation; he who gives, with liberality; he who leads, with diligence; he who shows mercy, with cheerfulness* (Romans 12:3-8).

Before exploring the spiritual gifts in more detail it is important to differentiate spiritual gifts from miraculous gifts. Miraculous gifts, such as speaking in a language that one has not studied or the gift of healing people were gifts that were given by the laying on of the apostles' hands. These gifts were used in the early church in part to demonstrate that the one sharing the message was in actuality a messenger of God and not a charlatan. Today we can investigate the scriptures to test the message of anyone who presents himself as a representative of God. If he does not speak the truths of the Bible, then we know he is a false teacher. In the early church, the writings of the New Testament had not yet been produced or collected, so those who proposed to speak on behalf of God utilized miracles to demonstrate that they were from God.

Spiritual gifts are given by God to each member of the body for the common good of the church.

> *Now there are varieties of gifts, but the same Spirit. And there are varieties of ministries, and the same Lord. And there are varieties of effects, but the same God who works all things in all persons. But to each*

> *one is given the manifestation of the Spirit for the common good* (1 Corinthians 12:4-7).

Spiritual gifts are not miraculous. They are not received by the laying on of hands. One is not able to do one day what he/she could not do the day before. Spiritual gifts are not given to offer validation from God. Spiritual gifts are given so that each person can find his place of service in the body. This is an ability that comes easily to the person who has received the gift. For instance, some members of the body receive the gift of teaching. Teaching seems to come naturally to them. Other members of the body would be scared to death if asked to teach because their giftedness lies in other areas.

Notice the gifts that are listed in the Romans 12 passage above:

Prophesy

Service

Teaching

Exhortation (Encouragement)

Giving

Leadership

Mercy

A whole book could be written about spiritual gifts and their use in the body. Such an investigation is beyond the scope of this book, however, for more investigation into the study of spiritual gifts, please refer to the resources listed at the back of this book.

Every spiritual gift is an ability in the rough. It must be identified and equipped for ministry (Ephesians 4:12). As we have seen, that is the role of those who are gifted with leadership, to help members of the body identify their gifts and then to construct a unique ministry utilizing that gift. This is where ministry gets exciting.

Imagine that receiving a spiritual gift is like waking up on your best ever Christmas morning. The greatest Christmas gift you have ever received is not one that you "ordered" for Christmas. Rather, it is a gift that was given to you by someone who knows you better than anyone else. When you opened the gift it was amazing because the gift fit you so well, even though it was not something on your list. That is how the Holy Spirit gives spiritual gifts. He knows you better than you know yourself, and does not give a gift you seek, but rather one that fits you to a tee.

It does not take much observation to conclude that there are different personalities that seem to go along with different skill sets. People with the gift of mercy tend to have different personalities than those with the gift of encouragement. Mercy is empathy, the ability to feel with someone. Encouragement is a cheer-leader, one who, as the word encouragement suggests, "builds courage into." One has a very soft heart. The other has a very strong will. They make a great team when someone is downfallen.

The mercy servant lets them know that they are not alone and that someone else knows their pain. Then the encouragement person helps to lift them out of the pain and depression they may be feeling. That person exudes a "you can do it, I'll be with you every step of the way" confidence that builds courage in the downtrodden member. Neither of these gifted ministers is a preacher (prophet), a pastor, or an evangelist, which are different gifts that involve different skill sets.

Professionalized ministry has prevented gifted ministers-to-be from ever realizing their destinies. At the same time, overworked (and under-gifted) professional ministers have teetered on the brink of burnout. That is a dysfunctional body. In fact, professionalized ministry has prevented many unequipped ministers-to-be from ever finding their destiny, the very reason they exist.

Each person is given a certain gift or set of gifts. Yet each person has a unique personality, a unique set of life experiences, and a unique passion for working with certain kinds of people. While others may possess the same gift of teaching that I possess, no one else brings to it the same personality, life experiences and worldview that I also possess. I am unique and my application of the gift of teaching will be unlike that of anyone else who has gone before or who will follow me. That total package makes my ministry unique. No one else will be able to minister to the people that I minister to in the exact same way that I can and will. I will reach a different set of people than you will, even if we have the same gift!

That is exciting. And that makes every gifted minister unique and irreplaceable. How horrible that millions have been relegated to the sidelines and have never been able to utilize their spiritual gifts in ministry. They have not realized their destiny.

Many Christians, having never been introduced to their spiritual giftedness, and having never been equipped for ministry by their leaders, have accepted roles as spectators in the body, a worship attender, a consumer. That is all they know to do. They then turn to other areas of their lives to give them meaning . . . careers, family, materialism, travel, shopping, hobbies, collecting, and on and on, believing that these things will validate them as human beings.

Not one of them is your destiny. Careers can be lost. Families can be taken away in a single accident, shopping is an unfulfilled hunger. There will be no careers in heaven. There will be no husbands, wives, sons and daughters. None of these is eternal, and therefore, merely temporal and not the foundation upon which to establish one's self-worth. In one hundred years the only two things that will matter is one's relationship to God through Christ and one's relationship with everyone else in the body of Christ (the people with which the saved will spend eternity.

Your place in the body is your destiny. That is what you were made for. It starts now, and it lasts throughout eternity.

If you have not found your ministry in the body, you have not begun to experience your destiny.

For too long the church has not been helping members find their destinies. We have children who rather than being born into a place in the body that gives them identity and a sense of destiny, have to look to peer groups, idols, or gangs to find a sense of validation. Our children should be just like Jesus, who at age twelve, in the Temple, knew exactly who he was and exactly what he was to be about.

Self-destructive behaviors that adolescents experiment with like drug and alcohol abuse, vandalism, rebellion, sexual experimentation, and the like in order to try to identify who they are, would not temp them, because of their fierce sense of destiny. Oh for a time when a couple at church has a baby and the whole congregation watches for signs of giftedness in that new child. They would plan how to plug her into ministry, so that she could grow up seeing everyone around her joyfully involved in ministry, much of it to her. She would find her validation in her unique ministry back to them. Her parents would never have to worry about her joining a gang someday because she would already have one!

Mutual ministry, built around each joint supplying its function, has been replaced by church work. Church work is usually someone having a dream for a program and then trying to recruit the whole congregation to get involved in it. Work is a four-letter word in most people's minds, even if the adjective church is put in front of it. It is because of church work that we have gotten so involved in trying to recruit volunteers to do what seemingly no one wants to do.

That is when we resort to bribes and guilt in order to motivate. Consider the following typical recruitment methodology:

Church Leader: *looking frantically through the foyer for a warm body.* Bob, we need a greeter at the front door this morning, would you be willing?

Bob: *who has the gift of administration and doesn't really like to interact with people.* I would rather you found someone else.

Church Leader: Well Sam was supposed to greet this morning but I just heard he is out of town and he didn't bother to tell me he wouldn't be here.

Bob: *feeling that Sam's absence didn't change his own desire to avoid interacting with people.* Why don't you ask Ralph to greet, he's not doing anything.

Church Leader: *getting frustrated because visitors are starting to enter the foyer.* Bob, you want to go to heaven don't you?

Bob: *wondering where this is going.* Uh, well, yeah.

Church Leader: Then get out there and greet. You know that a tree that bears no fruit will be cut down and thrown into the fire.

Bob: *reluctantly.* Well, okay, but you owe me one.

Church Leader: Thanks Bob, I knew I could count on you. I'll remember this when we vote for who gets the special 'servant of the month' parking space right by the front door!

Bob then wearily heads to the front door to do a mediocre job of leaving a first impression on newcomers to the assembly. Meanwhile, Church Leader heads off to find a warm body who can head up organizing the meal for the upcoming funeral service.

Most folks flee church work like moonshiners avoid revenuers. Everyone has been roped into doing something they don't like or feel inadequate about and that usually creates a negative experience. The "volunteer" then becomes gun-shy when the next opportunity emerges that requires volunteers. Church work has almost killed ministry in modern churches. The ministry for which God uniquely designed each individual person is built on a gift, not a curse. Servants who have been equipped in the use of their unique gifts bring refreshing attitudes to their ministries.

Terry is a technology person. He loves computers and such and would rather interact with them than with people. Terry was placed in charge of the audio/video production at church. He handles the lighting, sound, and video for the worship assemblies. Terry understands that he is one part of the body of Christ, and that when each minister fulfills their function, that body naturally grows as a result. Terry performs his ministry with a passion. He hand-picks and trains his co-ministers, based on their spiritual giftedness and passion.

Worship assemblies go off without a hitch. Terry makes sure. He spends endless hours preparing outlines, Power Point slide presentations, videos, wedding songs, lighting, funeral memorials, etc. He is worth his weight in gold. The ministry is self-perpetuating because Terry took hold of his destiny. Terry knows that when anyone is baptized, that he is a part. When anyone is consoled, he is a part.

Just like the shoulder that supports the elbow that moves the bow against the violin strings while the other hand fingers the neck, the result is beautiful music that all share in. It takes the involvement of each one to bring about any and every success. Terry is a poster boy for the difference between a gift-based ministering disciple and a guilt-motivated volunteer. Spiritual gifts are unique presents given to each Christian by the Eternal Gift Giver who knows each of them better than they could even know themselves.

When a Christian has found his destiny, his ministry is based on his unique blend of spiritual gifts, personality, life experience, and world view. Ministry becomes within him like a fountain that gushes forth a waterfall. Volunteers have to be continually extrinsically motivated. They draw energy (motivation) from another source, usually a church leader. That leader must then supply his own energy plus the energy drawn by volunteers. That is a winding-down energy system that will eventually run out of energy.

A burned—out ministry leader will be replaced by another ministry leader who will martyr herself in order to keep the volunteer system moving. Gift-based ministers are intrinsically motivated, for the Holy Spirit who indwells them is the power source for the utilization of the gifts that HE gave them. In fact, the best way to tell that a Christian has found his gift-based ministry is when you have to tell such a minister to take a break so that someone else can get a turn.

When I have spent whole weekends at congregations where I conduct seminars about how to help people locate their gifts and discover their ministries, I will have spoken for three hours on Friday night, up to eight hours on Saturday, and finished by speaking at the Sunday morning class and worship assembly. After speaking for 13 or more one-hour sessions in a weekend, I would travel back to my home congregation to preach on Sunday nights. My own folks would kid with me that they dreaded when I went away on a seminar weekend because I always came back so fired up that they couldn't get any sleep during the service. My body would be exhausted, but my spirit was on fire. Teaching and preaching are my two main spiritual gifts, and when I exercise my spiritual gifts, they do not run down my batteries. They charge them up!

No one had to beg me to go one more time. No one had to pump me up to fulfill my ministry because I have found my destiny! God wants the same experience for you . . . to discover your destiny and to plug it in to ministry that lights your fires of passion for service. That is God's gift to you, the grace of being able to serve in his kingdom, and to have FUN while you are doing it. It is a gift, not a curse!

The mythical Renaissance Man is the model upon which the philosophy of our whole educational system has evolved.

Leonardo Devinci is the golden child of western education. He was good at science, literature, art, invention, etc., a well-rounded, learned response to the ignorance and uncouthness of the Dark Ages. The reason we subject every student to a liberal arts education is because we are trying to make a Leonardo out of each one.

The ideal product of our antiquated educational system is a formal-dressed gentleman (or lady) who can discuss any topic at a party with depth, social grace and humor. The system works for multi-gifted children, who can be jacks of all (academic) trades, but it punishes single-gifted students who are gifted only in art, or science, or math, or geography, or humanities. There is actually a gift in the church that is like a jack-of-all-trades. It is the gift of 'helps.' Ministers with the gift of helps are able to serve in many different capacities. The rest of us shine in one or two areas.

How many young students have endured needless shame and embarrassment, not to mention scoldings and discipline, because they are forced to excel in areas in which they have no aptitude? All for a goal that God didn't even intend. In the church we do the same with preachers. They are supposed to have all of the spiritual gifts and to be able to lead in all ministries.

For centuries we have tried to train men for ministry to be Renaissance Ministers. Rather than understanding that a preacher functions as the tongue of the body, we expect him to function in the place of all body parts. Yet if he could do so, he would not need any other body part. He could do it all himself and he would not need anyone. He would only tolerate other Christians in the church.

No one has all the gifts, and no body part is any more important than others. They must work together and depend on one another in order for the body to function as a unified whole. The Renaissance Man and the Renaissance Minister models must die! They are killing ministry in the church. Body parts everywhere are decaying because the tongue is trying to do it all. But that cookie-cutter model is so strong, and has been around so long, that many will argue with the truth of God, that *all* members should be involved in _____ ministry (usually it is evangelism or visitation).

For decades churches have had leadership development programs like Pew Packers and Lads to Leaders in an attempt to make leaders out of each young person, regardless of who has or doesn't have the gift of leadership.

How many churches, rather than determining how many gifted teaches they have, and building their educational ministries around those ministers, break the congregation up into first grade, second grade, and third grade like the Renaissance-founded public schools, and let the number of classes drive how many "teachers" must be coerced into duty. Better to have mixed age classes taught by gifted teachers, than a predetermined number of classrooms filled with ungifted, indentured, warm-body volunteers whose lack of passion for education rubs off on the children at a very impressionable age. Children come standard with a passion to learn, but it doesn't take long for misplaced, ungifted (well-meaning) "teachers" to kill it.

Are you beginning to see how wide-spread the damage is from following wrong models rather than simply cutting gifted ministers loose to let the body naturally grow and flourish?

There is no determinism in the Holy Spirit's choice of what gifts to give to which Christians. There are gifts that some Christians receive, whose ministry we are all supposed to grow into. Hospitality is to be practiced by all Christians. All Christians are to grow in mercy. Yet those gifted with hospitality and mercy will usually always outdistance the rest of us in fulfilling that ministry because they were gifted by the Holy Spirit with that advantage. The rest of us have to learn. And the gifted ministers are the examples from whom we learn. If I am going to learn to be more merciful, who better to learn from than someone for whom mercy seems to come naturally?

Church Growth Crisis:
The Decline of Christianity in America

Part Three

Fulfilling the Great Commission: Churches That Won't

Chapter 8
Fulfilling the Great Commission

Churches That Won't:
The Inertia Church

Inertia is the desire of bodies in motion to continue in the same direction at the same speed unless acted upon by an external, unbalanced force. Once a movement, like Church Growth, gains speed and momentum, its default is to continue in the direction in which it is headed unless it is acted upon by anyone who would try to change the speed or trajectory of the movement.

When disciples of the Church Growth movement see the world through Church Growth lenses, the need for change becomes invisible. There is not so much a rebellion against reform as there is an inability to see fault or need. The inertia could be expressed this way:

1. Church Growth ideologies are the accepted way to grow a church.
2. If a particular Church Growth methodology is ineffective, it is because:
    a. It has not been implemented correctly (user error), or
    b. It needs to be replaced with a different Church Growth method.
3. If no Church Growth methodology is effective in growing the church, then the receptivity of the geographical location must be brought into question.

By its own definitions, Church Growth ideologies are unassailable because the possibility of ideological fault has been defined out of existence. Any system of beliefs that cannot be objectively invalidated cannot likewise be objectively validated. If the Church Growth ideologies are measured against themselves, they will always be internally, subjectively validated to the satisfaction of all those who wear Church Growth lenses.

When the strategies of the Church Growth movement are compared against the standard of the Bible, then they begin to fail.

There are three kinds of church leaders that will reject the information presented in this book (often without evaluation). The first category is comprised of churches that are being swept along by the church growth ideological inertia. Once a course has been chosen, it is easy to then switch to autopilot. This is especially tempting to churches that are directed by a board of some type. Boards are accustomed to dealing with crises, and the agendas of most board meetings are usually built around what crises are rearing, or trying to rear, their heads. This is a managerial approach to leadership rather than a visionary one.

The board members spend a few hours per week or month dealing with the emergent crises of the congregation. They attempt to deal with those crises and approve of what needs to be done in order to make it to the next board meeting. Such meetings are the duty of these duly elected officers, and the goal of the preparer of the agenda is to insure that the meeting is as efficient (short) and current (current crises) as possible.

This reactionary style of managing the church suggests that problem-solving is main purpose of the board. A board's perception of its purpose can be inferred from its functioning. Thus any ministry that is not presenting a problem is considered a successful ministry. This don't ask, don't tell policy functions well for that management style because evaluating ministries based on biblical definitions of success would most certainly raise problems. Problems raised are problems that have to be addressed in meetings, which results in longer meetings. The problem with this style of management is that it is not biblical:

Where there is no vision, the people perish (Proverbs 29:18)

What is most amazing about this non-evaluative church management style of leadership is that there is no accountability. How many board members of non-church boards of directors would be relieved of duty if they merely managed crisis. If church boards had a boss, most of them would get fired. But they do have a boss! It is God's "business" that these men are managing!

In order to evaluate success of any enterprise the following must take place:

1. Purpose/goal establishment
2. Outcome criteria measurement determination
3. Outcome evaluation.
4. Adaptation to bring outcomes more in line with goals.

Purpose/Goal Establishment

This is where many congregations start out on the wrong foot. Setting goals and purposes for the church is the business of the owner of the church, Christ Jesus. The biblical description Church of Christ is a statement of ownership. Only Jesus can establish what the church is to do and the criteria by which to determine if the church is doing so or not.

The problem with modern church leaders is that they treat the church as if it is theirs, rather than treating it as a divine stewardship of someone else's property. Size was never given by the Lord as the basis of determining success or failure. Faithfulness to his teachings always has been. There is no validation in size, only in faithfulness, but only as a result of a continual self-analysis of the church's practices evaluated in light of the teachings of scripture.

It is easy to fall into the trap of validation by numbers when the first part of Acts is read, which is the only place numbers are ever quantified. Church "membership" consisted of three thousand the first day, and before you know it, five thousand (Acts 4). Then the accounting of numbers disappears for the rest of the New Testament. Yet it was God who was adding people to the church daily as folks were being saved (Acts 2:47). So we see that Peter obeyed the Great Commission (preached the gospel, baptized them as commanded), and God added people to the church.

The number accounting was a demonstration that they were doing what they were commanded to do and that God was doing what only He can do. Human involvement in the growth of the church, from the perspective of the parable of the sower, is limited to casting seed everywhere. It is between the seed (gospel) and the soil (recipient) whether or not the seed will germinate. The sower cannot manipulate either the seed or the soil.

The basic Church Growth notion of receptivity is then a human attempt to manipulate the seed/soil interaction. The Church Growth scientist would determine that the path is unreceptive to the gospel and that sowing seed on the path is a waste of resources.

The Great Commission command was "all nations," all people. Jesus said nothing about preaching only to receptive nations. Paul shook out his garments at the Corinthian synagogue only after the Jews opposed and reviled him. He then announced that he was going exclusively to the Gentiles. Paul's methodology in a new city was to go to the synagogue first and then to the Gentiles. He was thrown out of many synagogues as in Corinth, but he was obeying what Jesus had commanded, "to the Jew first and also to the Greek" (Romans 1:16).

Paul did not determine the receptivity of any given synagogue, although history had taught him not to expect much. He knew it was not his call. His job was to obey and let God be God. The justice of God demands that the gospel be presented to the path (hardened soil) with no regard to the "success" or "failure" of its reception. Then no one can stand before God and claim that he never had opportunity to hear. It is not about the reception, it is about the opportunity to hear.

A look at the history of the growth of Christianity in the United States presents the startling reality that God's methodology of church growth has never been followed by mainstream churches. If you look at how Christianity spread throughout the frontier, it was often as a result of a traveling evangelist who preached for anywhere from weeks to months in a town where there was no church, or at least no representation of the evangelist's denomination. In these impromptu worship services, his fiery presentation produced "conversions" that created the local foundation of the newly planted church.

It was then the responsibility of the seminaries and universities to provide enough watering preachers to maintain the congregation of passive sheep who were not taught or expected to become ministering disciples. The concept of clergy and laity had come over on the Mayflower and the belief was never checked at the door to America.

In the recent past, many churches hosted revivals, tent meetings, brush arbor meetings, etc., as a major methodology of growing the church. These were basically additional worship services held throughout the week to invite neighbors to attend. These meetings were either held at the church building or off property, whichever was considered best for attracting non-members.

Those meetings, a culture/time based fad, gave way to the next fad as all fads do. But they did help to set the precedent for the current generation that inviting people to church was the major methodology for conversion. The methodology was never evaluated by scripture criteria, but rather on whether converts were made. Converts were made, but disciples arguably were not. The lack of biblical criteria insured that the methodology would be a fad.

Fast forward in your own personal history and reflect on the Church Growth methodologies whose utilization you have witnessed. The following are/were ways to get people to church:

1. Bus ministry
2. Marriage and family seminars
3. Campaigns (usually advertising a special speaker/ series).
4. Christian schools in the church building
5. Vacation Bible School
6. Church gymnasium (usually called anything but)
7. Mother's Day Out
8. Boy Scouts
9. Twelve-step programs
10. Other _____

All of these methodologies were intended to get folks into the church building or worship assembly in order to eventually convert them. In other words, since before the founding of this nation the church growth methodologies of Christendom have been "invitational." It is not surprising then that inviting someone to church or a church-related activity has been universally accepted as evangelism.

It was when Christian values began to wane in America, when those invitations were increasingly, politely turned down that the panic began. The evolution of invitational churches to attractional churches was a simple matter of acknowledging a competition among churches for a shrinking commodity (visiting worshippers).

None of this has anything to do with what God has called churches to do and church leaders to insure gets done. The brush arbors of yesteryear were merely the wind being sown that would result in the whirlwind of craziness in the assemblies that we see today in modern churches' pathetic attempts to out-attract all the other churches in town. None of it was commanded, expected, called for, implied, or suggested by God to his church.

We are products of human innovation and tradition that has blinded us to the fact that the whole system is corrupt and needs to be discarded and totally replaced. The second section of this book explored anew the Biblical teachings of the Bible concerning evangelism and discipleship. It is difficult to scrap your tradition in order to accept what is new, new in this case being 2,000-year-old truth that we have either not yet seen or not yet restored.

You now feel the same internal stress that the Jews of Jesus' day felt in the presence of his new teachings: follow him or stay with what you know, broken as it is. If church leaders are going to make the changes that are necessary in order to bring the congregation into full submission and obedience to God, the following must take place.

Establish an Outcome Criteria Measurement Determination

If the leaders of a congregation decide to change horses midstream and leave the traditions of men of the Church Growth movement to merely obey God, how will they know if they are being successful? Although as we have seen, size is never an indicator of success with God, it is such an easy measurement. That is part of its deceptive allure. Church leaders must develop criteria that they will use to insure that they are successfully completing their stewardship to God, for which he will judge them.

When the church at Pentecost obeyed God, he added people daily. They obeyed; God added. They didn't add people to the church; they obeyed what God told them to do. The criterion is simple obedience to God's Word. Noah preached for 100 years with no conversions. No preacher would want that statistic on his resume because church leaders will ask him for such statistical background with their CG lenses firmly in place. Noah would be infinitely "hirable" today, however, if the criterion were speaking the truth (obedience to what God had told him to do).

Our goal should be to open the New Testament to any part, read it, and then give an account to one another about how well we are obeying that scripture. If there are scriptures that we have ignored, then let's repent and get to work. Not easy, but simple.

Church leaders need to be prepared for uneasiness present in meetings when they give an open account to each other. We should much rather give an account to a group of our peers before we have to do so, alone, before Almighty God. If we are clinging to tradition, ignoring parts of the Bible that are uncomfortable, being negligent, being afraid, or being lazy, we need to get real with one another. At judgment, our next audit, God will be real, and he plays no games, be they social, denial, political or whatever.

The following, though often utilized, are not acceptable outcome evaluation criteria:

1. How we feel about what is happening.
2. How the media presents us.
3. How many or few there are of us.
4. How well our beliefs or methodologies jive with culture (philosophies of men). In fact, this should represent an inverse correlation.
5. Perceptions of whoever wants to vote on what outreach methodologies are utilized in the church.
6. Perceptions of whoever gives what amounts of money to the church.
7. How responsive non-regenerated minds are to our methodologies.
8. How attractive we are as a body or as a sub-group (youth, singles, single-again, golden-agers, etc.).
9. The state of our physical facilities (buildings, etc.).
10. Other _____

Outcome Evaluation

There is a corporate-board-like tendency among church leaders to believe that if someone is hired to perform a function or if a deacon is put in charge of a ministry then that responsibility is as good as fulfilled. Rarely do church leaders evaluate preachers, youth ministers, or "members" in light of the criteria for ministry that they are *supposed* to fulfill. Very few leaders even have evaluation criteria for such ministries/ministers. Usually ministers are retained or replaced as a result of how well liked they are. If members do not complain, then they can keep doing what they are doing. If members complain, rarely with a Bible-based charge against the minister, then the tenure of the minister is in trouble. This is one example of how politics has taken over true leadership.

In this post-Christian era in which we live, it is much more difficult to attract new prospects. The risk of disgruntled members (consumers) leaving the church because of dissatisfaction with ministers, based on their own subjective criteria, makes being a supported minister very dangerous. Holding supported ministers accountable to the subjective whims of consumers means there can be no reproof, correction, or convicting in the message or the teaching, because supported ministers can be replaced, but adherents are hard to get.

If church leaders evaluate themselves and everyone involved in ministry (which as we have seen is every "member"), then they have to be prepared for the time and effort involved in correcting ministry that goes awry. That is why the New Testament metaphor of shepherds is applied to church leaders rather than any metaphor of leadership by corporate board.

So many church boards have maintained such communicative distance from sheep for so long that the board members sense that there is a build-up of resentment among the sheep for being ignored or for having not been nurtured. Thus to begin to evaluate sheep in terms of their giftedness and ministry performance would be to open floodgates of resentment that would deluge them with complaints, problems, etc.

The reason that CEOs of corporations do not put themselves in the position of having to empathize with the workers in the plant is because if they do not experience the pressures and conditions employees work under, they do not feel a responsibility to those workers. Again, this is corporate denial by hiding behind the corporate shield in order to maintain a don't ask, don't tell policy that prevents working together as a whole. That is why the corporate world is often characterized as the working man and corporate official working against each other (union versus management).

Church leaders are afraid to open up the wounds that neglected sheep have carried for so long, because they fear the negative experience of the infection, the inflammation, and even the gangrene. If your congregation is governed by a board, in name or in function, dismantle it now! Replace it with a group of shepherds who will teach, nurture, admonish, and hold accountable the sheep given to their care.

Another reason why church leaders do not hold church members accountable for being ministering disciples is because of the concept of church members being volunteers. When the church is viewed on the same level as the Red Cross, the Optimist Club, or the Soup Kitchen, then its members will be viewed as volunteers. This is the problem with the term church *member*. The Bible uses the metaphor of a *body* having many members (parts), but the church is never described as being comprised of members.

The whole concept of membership is problematic. When we join a group we become a member. We add our membership to service groups, hospitals, and social agencies, as a choice we make. We choose to join and to unjoin. We choose to serve and when to serve, because after all, we are donating our time and effort. Our membership is under our control.

Disciples do not volunteer for service; they are inscripted. We are slaves, bond slaves. We were bought with a price. We were gifted by the Holy Spirit with spiritual gifts that he chose for us to use to the edification of the body. This is our spiritual destiny, not a choice we make.

Members of the body of Christ were once wild plants that were grafted into a holy root by God. The only choice we had in this matter was whether or not to accept the gospel of Christ. By obeying it, we were added to him by this marvelous process of spiritual grafting. He is then our LORD and KING and we are his servants, his slaves, his bond-slaves (slaves in bonds). Don't hear that preached too much in attractional megachurches do you? I do not know if American churches will ever be able to undo the damage that has been done by churches creating consumers of church resource goods rather than disciples (which is an upgrade word for slave), but the culture is headed to judgment while we are playing political correctness games with human souls.

When God judges this nation for its immorality and rejection of him, who do you think he will hold accountable for not telling them what he has told us to tell them? We will not even tell each other what he has told us to tell them. The wayward servant is always disciplined in biblical parables, and often it is to outer darkness with weeping and wailing and gnashing of teeth. The SERVANT is so judged in those parables, not the lost world.

A third reason that there is little accountability among board members or between board members and ministers (remember, that is everyone in the church) is in order to maintain what is called 'credible deniability.' Credible deniability means that any one leader or group of leaders can deny with full credibility any knowledge of anything that goes wrong. In like manner, a minister can be offered up as a sacrificial lamb.

In the corporate world, investor confidence is of utmost importance. When the company messes up, board directors can offer up a sacrificial lamb and demonstrate to the investors how the sacrificial lamb, usually in middle management, was able to deceive the board. That person can then be fired and the credibility of the board can be protected. It is rare when you will find the president of a Christian college stroll down the halls of the dormitories. If he does, he might see behaviors or decorations that do not represent the morality of the school. With that knowledge would then come a responsibility. That responsibility might lead to the eviction of a tuition-paying student, or a whole group of students, at a time when colleges are competing for student tuition. Remember that 'credible deniability' is still denial, and it holds no credibility with God.

Adaptation Necessary to Bring Outcomes More in Line with Goals

Since God expects a preacher to preach the whole counsel of God with teaching, reproof, correction, training, rebuking, and exhorting to a congregation then that should be the criteria by which his sermons are evaluated. That should be the criteria by which attacks against his sermons should be scrutinized. Church leaders should sit down with the preacher periodically and evaluate his performance based on the Biblical criteria for his ministry.

If it is found that the preacher has been avoiding certain biblical topics or that he has tended to become unbalanced by speaking about his hobby subjects, then a remedial plan needs to be established. He needs to be assured that every biblical subject and scripture needs to be addressed. Every sin that could cause a servant to lose his or her soul needs to be confronted using the Bible, regardless of who in the congregation may be involved in any given sinful lifestyle!

In the present political environment that envelopes most churches, any charge can be made against any preacher (or any other minister) without any criterial basis. He can be charged with being too dry, too comical, too deep, too shallow, too verbose, too compassionate, too insensitive, or any other of an endless list of personal dissatisfactions. Such charges deal with his presentation style, which is in part a product of his personality. His personality will rub certain other personalities the wrong way.

When such a charge is brought against a minister, the church leaders have no stated biblical criteria by which to judge his success at fulfilling his ministry, other than political ones, so each such charge must be entertained. Church leaders then usually try to soothe the disgruntled person in order to maintain "peace" (no political uprising). However if the person bringing the charge has enough political clout with the leaders (wealth, following, ability to cause trouble) then the minister's continued service may be jeopardized. If the minister has political clout (following, influence, money-backing) then a political war may result.

Sadly, the Bible has presented each ministry, along with the criteria by which to evaluate the success of that ministry. In the Old Testament, if the words of a prophet did not come true, then the prophet was stoned, regardless of how well-liked he was. We can know if an elder is completing his stewardship. We can know if an evangelist will stand before God blessed or cursed.

Those ministers who are not fulfilling their ministries need to be evaluated in light of scripture, and a plan for remediation needs to be created. That plan simply outlines the steps that the disciple must take in order to become a properly functioning member of the body of Christ. It is that plan development and evaluation of each congregational disciple that church leaders are to spend the greatest majority of their time involved in.

Based on the level of under functioning in which almost all of the church's disciples remain stagnant, the process may seem overwhelming. Remember that you are not alone. Ephesians 4:11 describes whole sets of leadership-gifted people that will help you to perform this task of equipping each joint to properly function in the body.

Once all of the remedial teaching and equipping work is done, the congregation will become a well-oiled machine that "builds itself up in love." Since the batteries of each of your disciple-ministers will be recharged through ministry rather than discharged, keeping people motivated will not be an issue. Then it is just a matter of fine-tuning a growing, self-building church. That kind of leadership is a joy!

Chapter 9
Fulfilling the Great Commission

Churches That Won't:
The "Successful" Church

The second type of church that will ignore the call to restoration found in this book is the self-perceived successful church.

The diagnostic utilized most frequently to gauge the success of Church Growth strategies is numbers. The numbers that are used most often as the major indicators of church growth success are attendance and contribution.

The attendance figure for the Sunday morning assembly (assemblies) is referred to most often as the measure of a church's health or growth. That figure usually also includes the attendance at Saturday evening assemblies of those churches that offer such services. Since CG is based on a pragmatic consideration of what works, that measurement would seem to be most telling. If an attractional church is focused on getting people to church (assemblies), then an increase in attendance at those assemblies would seem to provide validation.

How can the largest congregation in a city or in a denomination be wrong? How could a congregation that is hosting dozens of programs a week, whose parking lot seems to have cars in it day and night be considered anything other than successful? Easy, it simply depends on the standard used to evaluate success.

The charismatic pastor of the largest church in the largest of American cities worked hard his whole life to build a church that is a model for all others. He worked his way up, beginning at a small, rural congregation. He read the church growth books. He went to the lectureships, the church growth seminars, and was a disciple of the best and brightest minds on our Christian college faculties.

He added to all his training a willingness to take risks, an entrepreneurial spirit if you will. Rather than being satisfied by copying the ideas of other churches after the fact, he led a ministry staff that innovated ideas that other churches emulated. His calendar is filled with requests from other churches to teach them how to build such a large following with such great facilities. He has invested his whole life in getting to the top of his game. And that is the problem.

It is those with the greatest investment that have the most difficult time making the changes that they need to make. They are defined by their investment and their success by human standards. They are not defined by total submission to Christ or they would turn on a dime to more completely obey the will of God.

How could a congregation need to change . . .

1. . . . that has a preacher that is on a first name basis with presidents and celebrities?
2. . . . whose leader is seen on heavy rotation on television?
3. . . . when it takes in millions of dollars in contributions each year?
4. . . . when 100 new visitors attend its services every week?

5. . . . when the local civic groups check with the church's calendar before they plan any local events?
6. . . . when it has physical facilities that are worth more than $50 million?
7. . . . when it has state of the art technology and the classroom teaching resources that would pale any major university by comparison?
8. . . . when dozens of visitors ask to join the church each week?
9. . . . when it is opening satellite church campuses on a monthly basis?
10. . . . when it has a full-time staff in excess of 35 ministers?
11. . . . when it is featured in the local news broadcasts on a regular basis.
12. . . . when its church leaders are sought out for commentary when there is religious news coverage in town?

Such a congregation needs to change, not because of what it is doing, but because of what it is failing to do. The list of accomplishments above would be considered a success by most any observer, however, the standard of measuring success is misguided. Once those accomplishments are compared with what God has commanded all churches to do, those successes will be seen as what they really are, irrelevant.

If a military general orders a major to lead his company to the top of hill 470, it matters not what else that major and his company accomplish if they do not fulfill their field command. It will matter little if they were able to take hills 471, 472, and 473, if they disobey orders. If the major and his company are able to demonstrate great courage and discipline in battle, and complete objective after objective, the major will still face a court martial. He did not obey what he was ordered to do.

There is nothing wrong per se in any of the following activities:

>Bus ministry
>Marriage and family seminars
>Campaigns (usually advertising a special speaker/series)
>Christian schools in the church building
>Vacation Bible School
>Church gymnasium
>Mother's Day Out
>Boy Scouts
>Twelve-step programs
>Friend and Family Day
>-The list is endless-

The problem is when such activities become a substitute for what God has called the church to do. Only when church leaders have equipped all of its disciples to fulfill their ministries using the spiritual gifts given by the Holy Spirit can they turn to such strategies.

Any program or outreach that does not include functioning, gifted evangelists will not result in church growth. A Mother's Day Out ministry will not be effective in growing the church unless there are evangelists taking an active part in the ministry. Home-based small group Bible studies have been used by congregations for years in an attempt to grow, and most of them fail at that objective, because calling a small group evangelistic does not magically make it so. Such a group would need to have gifted and equipped evangelists, follow-up teachers, hospitality ministers, etc.

Once a congregation has equipped its members for ministry, the result is natural growth. Artificial programs and special facilities would be superfluous because all that is needed is gifted ministers in contact with needy people and ministry will automatically result.

It is the focus on the stuff and the facilities and the outlay of huge amounts of money that has taken the church's focus totally off what God has directed. That focus has been misdirected for so long that what is being espoused here sounds revolutionary, although it is 2000 years old!

While churches are entertaining and showering lost people with gifts in order to attract them to assemblies, the church nation-wide is shrinking! WHAT WE ARE DOING IS NOT WORKING! Can't we just admit that, cut our losses, and begin a back-to-the-Bible movement that will rectify all of this mess before it is too late for the United States of America?

It is sad that the churches that are on the cutting edge of this movement in the wrong direction will not face the reality of what they have wrought. The largest congregations in America, to which smaller churches have for decades looked for leadership, will continue their denial of reality. They will look to other fads and the madness will continue.

That is why there needs to be a grassroots movement among "average" congregations, whose "power" and "influence" are not on the line. Only congregations that will not confuse success by any other standard than complete obedience to God will be willing to let all the trappings go.

All major, history-changing movements that have turned things around have begun as grass roots movements. They have caught fire and taken the power and influence brokers by surprise, because once leaders become successful, they have a lot invested in the status quo.

The standard for "success" in Christian ministry can never be established by anyone other than Christ Jesus, whose owns this church with which we are concerned. The failure of any church or individual cannot become justification for the failure of any other group or individual.

If the largest churches in America are failing at completing God's will for them, that does not justify your or my failure or the failure of the congregations with which are associated. That is the problem with the 'growth strategy via peer pressure' approach of the past.

The leaders of most congregations look to what other churches are doing in order to establish their ministry strategies. If the strategies that a large congregation is using appear to be working (pragmatism), then they are copied. If one church gets a bus, the others get a bus. If one church starts a Mother's Day Out program, then the peer congregations do as well.

Looking to other churches rather than looking at scripture over and over and over again is what has led to the decline in Christianity. Instant media and religious publications and websites have fueled this competitive vortex.

Christian colleges and church growth gurus, feeling the pressure to be on the cutting edge in order to present the church's answer for why nothing is working, succumb to the same pressures and to quickly falling for the next fad. If a Christian college is going to stay on the forefront, then it must adapt the latest fads immediately, or risk falling behind and being viewed as irrelevant and old fashioned. The pressures, and thus the pitfalls, are enormous.

Do not expect the "leaders" in the field of Church Growth to lead the return to the Bible movement that this nation and its churches need. Don't expect to witness it at lectureships or on Christian college campuses, unless it is student led.

Billy Mitchell was the first American to fly over an enemy during war. Billy had been a colonel in charge of air support in World War I. The airplane had been just invented and what Billy first flew was little more than wood and canvas with an engine about as powerful as a lawnmower's. Billy envisioned a future for the use of aircraft that would shorten wars and thus casualties.

The army, with their cannons and a long tradition of fighting on battlefields and trenches had no use for Billy's heretical ideas. The Navy, with its massive battleships and stealthy submarines, scoffed at Billy's vision of an Air Force. Even though he hosted amazing demonstrations of the ability of airplanes to sink the largest ships with ease, both services were so steeped in their tradition and lack of vision that they refused to anticipate the future of war. By the time that Hitler was amassing his visionary military forces to, General Billy Mitchell was outright persecuted by the military branches. He took his case to the American people.

Billy was a powerful spokesman for establishing air superiority in war. The highest ranking officials in the Army and Navy warned him to stand down. Billy warned of a rising Japanese threat to Hawaii. In 1926, fifteen years before the attack on Pearl Harbor, Billy not only warned of the impending threat, but all but demanded that America needed to design aircraft that could respond to such a threat. The military had the budget resources to do so. He pleaded with the political leaders of the armed forces to see what was happening in warfare. They responded by pressuring President Calvin Coolidge to order Billy's court martial. Billy died a broken man six years before the attack on Pearl Harbor and the beginning of the massive loss of life in the Pacific war. "The American people will regret the day I was crucified by politics and bureaucracy," was one of his last recorded statements.

The story of General Billy Mitchell's clear vision and prophesy was probably not included in your education in American history. It is not only an embarrassing chapter in military history, but it places the guilt for unnecessary loss of life at the feet of the very leaders whose responsibility it was to prevent such travesties. It is understandable that Billy's story has been swept under the historical carpet.

Maybe in a sense the military and political leaders of Billy's day can be forgiven for their failing. History tends to judge harshly what at the time could have been viewed as at best a gamble. Billy was a visionary and they were traditionalists. He tried to get them to share a vision of what became a paradigm shift in how wars were to be fought. Rarely are leaders visionary.

Many modern church leaders are falling into the same trap as those powerful World War II dignitaries. In our case, however, it is not a matter of failing to be visionaries. As noted, few ever are. Our responsibility is not vision, but rather obedience. Most of the time our attempts to be visionary (innovative) get in the way of our call to be simply obedient.

At judgment, will God hold the persecutors of Billy Mitchell responsible for the needless death of tens of thousands? Only he knows. But if God himself had commanded the American military to build an Air Force that would give them air supremacy and thus prevent or quickly end the war in the Pacific and they failed to do so, they would call of mountains to fall on them at judgment.

The church and Christianity are in decline in America. God has given us all that we need to stem the tide and turn it around. We are not listening. The lives of soldiers are not at stake here. The souls of precious men, women and children are at stake. The consequence of failure, or rather negligence, is judgment by God himself. Please wake up!

Chapter 10
Fulfilling the Great Commission

Churches That Won't:
The "Bunker" Church

Ironically, one of the most dangerous classifications of non-growing churches is the church whose leaders oppose the consumer-producing, marketing methodologies of the attractional churches. These leaders are either able to spot the biblical fallacies at the foundation of the Church Growth Movement, or they are simply mired in tradition and avoid those pitfalls as a product of inactivity and unwillingness to change. These bunker churches are inward oriented. The best of these service and maintain their members with programs, support groups, Big Events, seminars and other activities that give the impression of movement. Most are merely treading water and working hard to maintain their memberships.

While visitors are welcome and even treated as honored guests, they are not actively sought. If a visitor wants to become a part of the church, the visitor must conform to the ideologies and methodologies of the congregation. In bunker churches, the congregation has confused the hierarchy of service. The church (organization) serves its members and the members have "tenure." New members must submit to an unspecified amount of time on "probation" before membership status is fully conferred. Of course these words are never used, and the congregation is not even aware that these informal, unspoken rules are in place, but an outsider can perceive them.

Leadership v. Politics

Possibly the greatest reason that church leaders will find it difficult to follow the biblical vision presented in this book is that leadership has been replaced by politics. The attractional model of the Church Growth Movement is based on meeting the desires of consumers (marketplace). One of the earliest of the megachurches is a group that started quite small, and grew by presenting to outsiders what outsiders wanted to see in church. They actually surveyed the neighborhood and asked those who did not attend church why they didn't.

The folks surveyed stated that they didn't like traditional church music, so the congregation changed its music to meet the desires of the "unchurched." Those respondents also reported that they didn't like preaching, so drama and a short, uplifting conversational message were substituted. In short, they polled lost people to see what would attract them to church and adjusted their practices to meet those expressed desires.

Throughout history the church has been bombarded by those who would change her teachings in order to suit the desires of certain sets of people. That attack has generally come from within, by religious leaders who try to quell the desires of religiously wandering members. Church designed and structured by pagans for pagans brings a whole new application of Jesus's warnings about the substitution of God's word for human precepts.

> *This people honors me with their lips, but their heart is far away from me, but in vain do they worship me, teaching as doctrines the precepts of men* (Matthew 15:8-9).

On behalf of marketing the church, church leaders in essence empowered lost people to design worship. That makes brilliant marketing sense, but the church is not a marketplace, and humans are not free to build worship to fit their own liking. But that is state of the art in most modern congregations today, to one extreme or another. As noted earlier, for the most part, the history of Christendom in America is that attraction has almost exclusively been the tool of "outreach."

In the present culture of church shopping, church leaders understand that if they do not cater to the desires of "seekers" then some other church will. Bunker churches that may not be as oriented toward attracting seekers, and who may feel a sense of superiority because they have not "sold out" to pandering for members, still feel the pressure of keeping their own members happy in order to not lose them. Leaders in such churches need not feel that they are different, because they are succumbing to the same attractional pressures, even though they are using attraction to keep members rather than to win members.

The result of this ubiquitous marketing pressure is that there has been a dumbing down of discipleship that is systematically eradicating the very meaning of the term, and thus the very concept that is the basis of our relationship with Christ. If our interaction with Christ is based on a non-biblically define relationship, then there are serious problems in our church culture.

Leaders fear that if they treat members as disciples (slaves to a King) rather than marketing to them as shoppers and consumers, that they will experience the sum of all of their fears. They fear that the members will leave and find a church that caters to their "felt needs." Then the contribution will free fall. With a declining contribution, the staff will have to be let go, one at a time, until there are no supported ministers. This creates a cycle of decline for which there is no solution. Less members giving means less staff, which means less ministry to members, which means less members, which means less contribution, which means less staff . . . believe me, that is the way boards of directors talk behind closed doors.

The finality of this envisioned dooms-day scenario which, ironically, would be brought about by obeying the Bible rather than the philosophies of men, is that the group eventually would shrink so small that it must sell the building, and disband. The loss of the building would really mean the loss of identity as a church. That is what leaders fear will happen if they treat members as disciples not as consumers.

The fears of human leaders will not be realized when God is completely obeyed. Granted, there will be costs associated with a fundamental change of vision and direction for the church. But that will be a function of how far the church has wandered from truth and how long the associated sins have been allowed to grow and function as leaven in the church.

Jesus promised that he will be with us every step of the way when he gave us the Great Commission as our church growth mission. That means that our fears, as stated above, will never be realized while God is at the helm. However, like an ailing tooth, it is how completely and quickly we respond to the decay that determines how disruptive the reconstruction will be. If the cavity in a tooth is discovered during a preventive visit to the dentist, it can usually be taken care of right then with minor discomfort. That is the benefit of being proactive rather than crisis oriented.

If the decay is allowed to grow undetected, it will destroy increasing parts of the tooth. Once it gets to the nerve, which is deeply embedded in the tooth, an alarm is sounded (ache!). If the alarm is ignored or treated as a symptom, then the damage to the nerve will kill it and stop the pain. Then the tooth may become impacted as the infection moves to the surrounding gum. At this point if pain drives us to the dentist, the problem cannot be dealt with because of the surrounding emergencies that the original problem has caused. Now the dentist must prescribe an antibiotic to reduce the swelling of the gum so that the needs of the tooth can be fulfilled. By this time, the discomfort and expense associated with curing the problem have grown immensely.

During the time that the tooth is impacted, if one takes pain killers (prescribed by the dentist to alleviate pain until the swelling goes down) to kill the pain associated with the infection, and the infection is treated by the antibiotics, then the pressure on the nerves in the gum will be eased, allowing the dentist to work on the tooth, or allowing the tooth to once again be ignored. If the tooth is again ignored, then the future holds root canals, crowns, bridges, implants, dentures, jaw bone replacement, cancer, etc. The earlier the problem is detected and the more complete the intervention, the less the pain and expense in the future.

If you are a leader in an attractional church, and you have been convicted by the biblical teachings in this book, there will be no better time than right now to lead a reform movement in the congregation to return to God's teachings, his power, and his blessings. The further you have gone down that road, and the more consumers you have attracted, the greater will be the apparent loss. Many consumers will leave when called upon to become biblical disciples of Christ.

Many followed Jesus into the desert to see his magic show and to receive healings or food from him, and many left when he taught that to be his disciples they would have to eat his flesh and drink his blood. So many of them left that Jesus asked his disciples if they were going to also leave. Peter replied that they had no place to go, because Jesus alone had the words of life (John 6:68). Folks will leave. Maybe a lot of folks will leave. Those who leave are followers, but not disciples. Remember, they were not disciples because they were taught to be selfish consumers. We were taught that that is how the church grows in America. And they consumed everything that was offered freely, didn't they?

A church cannot be built on consumers. A church can only be built on disciples who are willing to take up their crosses and die for their Lord and King (Matthew 16:24). The rest were sent there by Satan to water down the teaching, the giving, the commitment, the service, and the spirit of unity.

As your attractional church "grows" you find that you can do less and less. You are hampered in what you can teach, you can never have enough paid staff to meet the needs of the consumers (more consumers means more consumption, and it is exponential in its growth). There are times when you wish you could go back to the days when you were first called. You had so much passion for Christ that you would have happily gone to your death for him. Then you became a victim of the Church Growth Methodologies that were presented by the Church Growth Gurus who were supposed to be telling you what was right. You trusted them and seemed to have success as more shoppers chose your congregation to make the home of their consumption, as long as the consumables were better than they were at the up and coming church down the street.

It all became so complex, and you wish for the simplicity of a church that was not an enterprise but rather a naturally growing organism. You can return to that simplicity and freedom, and lead a revolution that will change not only your church, but the community, the state, and the nation.

Pruning a tree of its dead wood as a growth strategy is not only natural it is a biblical metaphor. You have dead wood that needs to be pruned. You don't prune them by kicking them out, you prune them by confronting them in what they are doing and calling them to repent. You confront their consumerism and immorality and call them to the repentance and confessions that are hallmarks of the disciple's life. If they are there for the magic show and the freebees, they will quickly leave. If they stay and are rebellious, that is the purpose of discipline (Matthew 18). Remember, discipline and disciple share the same root word. They are cognates of one another. Disciples respond very well to discipline; goats do not. Jesus will separate the sheep from the goats at his return.

Your congregation will do more with a 100 devoted disciples than it will ever do with 3000 self-oriented consumers. Just imagine what 3000 disciples could accomplish in self-denying service to one another and to the lost. You would not even need a staff. You would never have to ask for money again. You would never have another giving drive because disciples give from the heart as part of their sacrificial lifestyle. They give to God as part of their normal service, not to a budget or a building program! Jesus focused on discipling twelve men for his whole ministry and those twelve men changed the world.

Then what do church leaders do, who have read to this point in the book and are convicted by their responsibility to equip members of the body for ministry? The first step is to repent to the congregation in sack cloth and ashes. This is not a challenge for shepherds but it is abhorrent to directors of the board, who hide behind a corporate shield rather than to ever admit error.

David, who was not only a shepherd by trade, but who had the heart of a shepherd is a great example of a leader after God's own heart. David made many mistakes during his reign, such as:

1. Uzzah's death when the ark was moved at David's command.
2. Adultery with Bathsheba.
3. Murder of Uriah, Bathsheba's husband.

4. Death of 70,000 faithful servants because David took a census and angered God.

Yet God described David in the following way after his death:

> *and tore the kingdom away from the house of David and gave it to you-- yet you have not been like My servant David,* **who kept My commandments and who followed Me with all his heart, to do only that which was right in My sight** (1 Kings 14:8)

All of David's sins God forgot because David did such a great job with repentance. David even led the whole nation in repentance when such was appropriate. Political leaders today deny and divert and only admit error when they are caught by the media and can no longer deny. There is no media to hold church leaders accountable to obedience to the words of God. Unless they hold each other accountable, the next accountability is to God himself at judgment. That is a sobering reality!

Next the congregation is to be called to repentance. The congregation cannot be called to repentance until the leaders lead in repentance. Real leaders never call their followers to do what they will not lead them in doing. David led the nation is repentance. David was not ashamed as king to repent in humility before Israel. That is why he was the greatest king of God's holy people, ever, until Christ came, the only sinless, mistake-proof leader.

Get ready for many to leave. Get ready for the disciples who follow the leaders in repentance to be galvanized into a spiritual machine that is ready to fight the spiritual battle in front of us with passion and commitment you have never witnessed in an attractional church. Trust God. His ways work. After the pain of the course correction and the burning away of the dross that is the consumerism, you will be in position for God to do amazing things. The things that he has promised to do.

> *All authority (and power) has been given to me in heaven and on earth, go therefore, and preach the gospel . . . and lo, I am with you always, even to the end of the age (Matthew 28:18, 20).*

There is authority, power, and promise in that command!

Once the leadership and congregation have repented, it is time for a new course. The pure consumers have left. Some consumers have been convicted, and have become disciples. The disciples, probably the core that the church had all along been built upon, are energized. Everyone is on the same page. That page is the Bible. It is now time for a return to the Bible. That no longer means sermons using the Bible as a back-drop for pithy stories and feel good sentiments. Refer to chapter one for a review of what real preaching and teaching looks like.

If you simply do not know where to start, there are resources listed at the back of this book that will help you move from shallow, experience-based preaching and teaching to the real meat of the Word. They are worth investigating. The resources that help disciples discover, identify, and make ministry out of their spiritual gifts will save you a lot of time trying to reinvent the wheel.

Biblical leadership does not come through committee. Bible leadership comes down to one man taking a stand for God. This does not happen by agreement with others, it happens as a conviction deep within the one who must often stand alone. But don't elders represent leadership by group? Yes, in vision, but not in conviction. Moses stood alone, often against his own people, the people he was called to serve (lead). Other leaders of Israel rebelled against him, even his own brother and sister.

Nehemiah stood alone. The dispirited nation drew its strength from him to rebuild the wall of Jerusalem. Jeremiah and Ezekiel stood alone, and were punished for it. In fact, Stephen accused the forefathers of the Jewish counsel of killing all of the prophets (Acts 7:52). Paul died alone. Jesus went to the cross alone. All the disciples but John had abandoned him, Peter denied him three times! Biblical leaders stood not on convention of decision, but on character and courage of inner conviction and obedience to God.

We do not draw courage to lead from associates. That must come from within. Once men of personal courage and conviction come together, they are then able to forge a vision that is both true to God and courageous. Corporate men hide. Men of God stand . . . out front! Boards use secrecy and anonymity to avoid responsibility for decisions. Elders lead from the front (sheep cannot be driven from behind).

Moses was chosen by God because he was a true leader. His meekness meant that he was not trying to be popular or accepted by people. It also meant that he would completely obey God and not depend on his own strength or ability.

Charlton Heston is one that Hollywood would cast for leadership of Israel. The Charlton Hestons end up getting into competition with God (King Saul, Solomon) because they are strong personalities that take great pride in their strength. Godly leaders find their strength and conviction in God alone. Only then are they ready to be a part of a leadership team.

Aaron, Moses' choice for the leadership of Israel, was a better politician but a horrible leader. When Moses was on the mountain receiving the law from God, the people pressed Aaron into building a god to lead them from the wilderness. Aaron gave the people what they wanted out of fear of the people. He wanted to be liked by them, to be followed by nature of his charisma with them. He led the nation into rebellion against God. He claimed it was not his fault; it was the people who were difficult to get along with. Aaron was a coward. Politics creates cowards.

Think back on the two choices for leader: Moses, who obeyed God to the point of making the people drink the water that contained their melted god in it, or Aaron, who gave them what they wanted. Who would the search committee of an attractional church choose for its pulpit? As the result of such an interview, Moses, Noah, Jeremiah, Ezekiel, and Paul would be rejected. They would have trouble finding a place to preach today.

God's true prophets would have to find another line of work today, and pulpits everywhere would be filled with Aarons. American churches are not victims of religious decline in the United States; we are the perpetrators. Are you beginning to see the scope of the leadership problems we have today? It was so bad in Amos's day that God had to go outside the prophets, priesthood, and leadership of Israel to find someone who would tell his people the truth (*I am not a prophet or the son of a prophet, Amos 7:14*). Please take off your lenses and look long and hard at this message, not in terms of how it makes you feel, or what you may have to lose, but in terms of how true it is to the Bible. Be courageous and do what is right.

Most groups that lead are codependent to the group's own weaknesses rather than functioning according to God's desire, as iron sharpening iron. What should precede the repentance of the leadership as they lead the church in its course change is a self-reflection of each leader and accountability within the group to assess if each one even has the gift of leadership. A change may be needed, based on the giftedness of each one.

The longer the church has been attractional, the greater the possibility that politicians were chosen to lead the church.

Often men are chosen for church leadership who have been successful in business or community leadership (politics) and the qualifications that made them successful in those arenas may be what actually disqualifies them from leading the church. The "qualifications" for elders and deacons are character descriptions, not business or political shrewdness.

The leadership structure of the church is a Christocracy. The church has one head, Christ. He died for the church, it is his bride. He bought it with his blood. The name Church of Christ (Christ's Church) shows ownership and is in possessive form in English and Greek. Preachers, pastors, elders, and deacons do not establish policy for the church. They are rather stewards who are supposed to apply Christ's directions to Christ's church ("teaching them to obey all that I have commanded you," Matthew 28:20).

Americans live in a democracy (okay actually a representative republic, but this is not a civics lesson) and we hold freedom of choice and rule by the people as cherished notions associated with our political freedom. The problem is that Christians bring democratic notions to church. The church is not a democracy.

It is worth asking that if democracy is the greatest form of government then why didn't God ever utilize it. God never used democracy as the form of government that he established with his people. That is because sheep cannot lead themselves. They need a shepherd, not another sheep, to lead them. You don't get to vote about what the church will or won't, should or shouldn't, do. Nor do the leaders.

Leaders of bunker churches speak long and hard about the errors of the attractional churches. They believe that they are justified by not catering to the selfishness of lost "seekers" while they use political leadership styles to keep their attendees in attendance through using the same attractional gimmicks, only as inreach maintenance, not outreach growth. They use technology, drama, gymnasiums, engaging sermons, special music, etc. in order to keep their easily distracted attendees from being attracted to the church down the street. They don't lead, they acquiesce to fear.

The bunker church is led by fear. Actually it is fear that prevents the "leaders" from leading. They are afraid of trends, and they are afraid of change. They are afraid of the problems that will come into the church if many lost people are converted. They are afraid that the church doesn't even have enough resources for the members, let alone for those who have been immersed in the soul-robbing, sinful lifestyle of the world.

Bunker churches are proud of the fact that they are not attractional churches; however, they are using some of the same church growth strategies to be **preservational** churches. As misguided as attractional churches are in their methodologies, at least they are attempting to be proactive in reaching out to (or inviting in) the lost. Preservational church leaders accept Church Growth methodologies that they learn from attractional churches in order to react to the growing impatience of their own attendees. When preservational church leaders realize that young parents are leaving the church in order to attend an attractional church that offers great programs for children, the bunker church will grudgingly build a gymnasium in order to stem the exodus or to try to get their former attendees back. In reacting to the pressure placed upon them by unhappy members, they demonstrate that they do not lead at all. They follow the pressure.

The very people who are able to present a great enough crisis to get bunker church leaders to make a change do not respect their own leaders. They know that such crisis management style is not leadership, even in the world. The members who watch the leaders acquiesce to the political pressure of the dissatisfied, squeaky wheels in the church do not respect the leaders either. They know that the leaders are being manipulated by the followship, which means that the followship is really the leadership, and the leadership is 'leading' by following the desires of the disgruntled.

Maybe, just maybe, if bunker church leaders will return to simply following the teachings of the Bible, God's wrath against this nation, against a church that has lost its way and ventured beyond his call, can be diverted. Then a revival, the likes of which this nation has never seen, will sweep this country like wildfire, bringing Jesus as Lord back into the hearts of ever American man, woman, and child. Then morality will be restored to our lives, and then to our schools, politics, and society, because we will once again be servants of Christ Jesus, not self-absorbed consumers seeking something else to devour, to our destruction.

Church Growth Crisis: The Decline of Christianity in America

Part Four

Fulfilling the Great Commission:

Churches That Didn't

Chapter 11

Fulfilling the Great Commission

Churches That Didn't: Judgment

It is Judgment Day. The church leaders from your congregation are standing before the judgment bar of God. As the name of the day represents, this is the day on which every person who has ever lived will be judged by God. Some will leave that judgment and go with him to live in eternity in heaven; most will not. Judgment Day is about justice. Many people misunderstand the fact that Jesus first came to earth in one capacity, but that he will be returning in another. Both roles represent the justice of God. In speaking of his first coming, Jesus stated:

> *And if anyone hears My sayings, and does not keep them, I do not judge him; for I did not come to judge the world, but to save the world. He who rejects Me, and does not receive My sayings, has one who judges him; the word I spoke is what will judge him at the last day* (John 12:46-49).

The second coming will be very different. Paul describes the scene the next time Jesus visits the cosmos:

> *. . . when the Lord Jesus shall be revealed from heaven with His mighty angels in flaming fire, dealing out retribution to those who do not know God and to those who do not obey the gospel of our Lord Jesus. And these will pay the penalty of eternal destruction, away from the presence of the Lord and from the glory of His power, when He comes to be glorified in His saints on that day, and to be marveled at among all who have believed-- for our testimony to you was believed* (2 Thessalonians 1:7-9).

The next time we see Jesus will be on the Day of Judgment, in which he will return to judge, with vengeance, those who have not obeyed him.

The judgment encounter is best visualized as taking place in a courtroom. While each church leader will be rewarded or sentenced independently of the others, in matters of leadership they may all testify together, since justice demands that no one can blame another or take responsibility for another's good deeds. It will all be settled right then and there. Each of their testimonies will be validated or repudiated right there. All of their discussions, meeting minutes, decisions, agreements, disagreements, acts of leadership, acts of cowardice, and upholding or withholding of the teachings of the Bible will be laid bare.

Sins of weakness and human failure will be covered by the grace of God, administered by the gospel of Christ Jesus. Sins of neglect or rebellion against the will of God, as revealed by the Word of God, will be judged, as they always have been in scripture.

Just like in an earthly courtroom, things are rather formal, because souls are at stake. Charges will be read, laws appealed to, and admission of evidence will occur because there is no justice unless every "t" is crossed and every "i" dotted. Nothing will escape notice, and nothing will be hidden, for there will be no future appeals.

One of the most deeply impressed images on my memory is of my earthly father enforcing accountability for his commands. I do not recall ever seeing my father lose his temper. If he ever yelled at me when I disobeyed him, I have no memory. My father was an even tempered man who let the authority of his words stand on their own.

My father did not beg me to do chores or remind me and remind me of what he had told me to do. He stated his directive once, made sure his command was understood, and then held me accountable for obeying it. It was understood, unless dad placed a deadline on a directive, that it was to be accomplished immediately.

More than once I would tarry after a command. Maybe I was in the middle of a made for TV movie, yearning to find out 'who done it.' Dad would enter the room and ask in a measured, controlled voice, "Son, what did I tell you to do?" When I heard those words I knew I was busted. No deals would be struck, no excuses would be accepted. I would be disciplined for negligent disobedience.

The fact that dad never raised his voice or threw a temper tantrum made the justice of his discipline so clear. I was not being disciplined because he was mad or because he was having a bad day. I was being disciplined because I was disobedient to my father, even though I was not trying to be rebellious, just trying to see the rest of the movie. I followed my will, not his.

I envision God passing out discipline on judgment day in a manner not unlike my father's. The preaching of grace to the exclusion of obedience has created a sense of license among God's people. God will forgive everything. Even rebellion and neglect. God gave us commands and directives, not in order to offer us a foundation for disobedience, but that we might love him enough to try to act like he would in any given situation. Grace has become the license for many to ignore the teachings of God!

Many church leaders will stand before God and hear him ask, "Son what did I tell you to do?" We will then give an account for every action, every word spoken. He will ask, "Did you give it your best effort?" If the answer to that question is yes, but that the efforts failed, his grace will cover that weakness. If the answer to the question, verse by verse, commandment by commandment, is 'no,' then he will ask if we understood the command. Was it revealed in the Word? Was it clear? Was it confusing? What will we say?

Many church attenders will stand before God and hear him ask them, "Son/daughter, what did I tell you to do?" He will ask if they completed their ministries. He will ask if they fulfilled their part of church growth: *from whom the whole body, being fitted and held together by that which every joint supplies, according to the proper working of each individual part, causes the growth of the body for the building up of itself in love* (Ephesians 4:16). As things stand right now, most of them will not even know what he is talking about, much less be able to defend their level of obedience.

He will ask them if they understood the command. Was it revealed in the Word? Was it clear? Was it confusing? He will not ask those questions to be cute or cynical, but rather because justice demands them. What will they say?

He will then ask the preachers whether or not they warned the "disciples" that God would hold them accountable for his instructions about the use of their spiritual gifts in ministry. If the preachers cry out that they tried and tried, but that no one would listen, then his grace will cover them. If the preachers say that they had never been taught such teachings, then God will then ask if they had a copy of the Bible available to them. Was it revealed in the Word? Was it clear? Was it confusing? Then the blood of those disobedient disciples will be visited on the preachers.

The blood of the disobedient disciples and the negligent preachers will then be visited upon the church leaders, for it is their responsibility to . . .

Be on guard for yourselves and for all the flock, among which the Holy Spirit has made you overseers, to shepherd the church of God which He purchased with His own blood. I know that after my departure savage wolves will come in among you, not sparing the flock; and from among your own selves men will arise, speaking perverse things, to draw away the disciples after them (Acts 20:28-30).

Epilogue

This book contains many challenges to the status quo of declining Christianity in the United States of America. The most troublesome has been left for last. The history of God's people describes many more descents into apostasy and rebellion than restorations like Josiah's. Even in the case of Josiah, as soon as he died the people reverted to their ignorance of the Word of God and to the worship of idols.

God's greatest tool for attempting to return his people to himself was bondage. Historically the church has grown like wildfire in the face of persecution and intense opposition. God's people have never done well in times of prosperity. It seems to be the opposition from the evil one for which we have not found an antidote.

When Israel was about to cross the Jordan river to the land that flowed with milk and honey, God warned them that when they no longer had to depend on him directly for manna like in the wilderness that they would soon forget him. They did.

When we are comfortable and our bellies are full, it is difficult for us to find the motivation to leave our couches of comfort and submit ourselves to the pain of any amount of self-discipline or training. Since self-discipline is part of the fruit of the Spirit, then our lack of a burning desire for self-discipline demonstrates that we are not spiritual people. We have become carnal, giving in to the gratification of our senses, while attending church services and taking the Lord's Supper.

There are no alarms being sounded. The church is in decline while we are giving away trinkets to try to get people to come to our assemblies. We have reduced the number of our assemblies and Bible studies because our "disciples" have voted with their absence, that they have enough, thank you.

It may be that the warnings in this book have come years or decades too late. It may be that not only in our culture, but in our own congregations that . . . *there is no fear of God before their eyes* (Romans 3:18).

When God told Ezekiel to warn God's people of the captivity that was looming over them if they did not repent and turn back to him, it was already too late. It was not too late to turn, for that is never the case. It was too late for them to want to turn.

Church leader, preacher, disciple, what will you do with the message of this book? It matters not that you agree with all or part of it. What matters is what you do with what you have learned or been reminded that is true. Remember the warning of James:

> *Therefore, to one who knows the right thing to do, and does not do it, to him it is sin* (James 4:17).

You need a plan: a plan for how to begin a restoration in your own life, a plan for how to share the restoration in your life with those who are disciples at the church where you serve . . . a plan for calling the leaders in your church to repentance and obedience. You need help. The next section of the book will offer resources that can help you do what you know you need to do. This may be the very destiny to which you were created!

Please do not put this book down without some kind of resolve for some kind of a plan. Please!

Also Available:

Why Churches Aren't Growing

A Bible Class and Small Group Study Curriculum Companion to
Church Growth Crisis

www.churchgrowthcrisis.com

Resources

Consulting

Stephen Parker will serve as a consultant to your congregation in order to assess the changes that need to be made to become a biblically growing congregation, and he will work with your church leaders to develop a step-by-step plan to achieve that turnaround. Parker has worked with dozens of churches who are attempting to restore New Testament structure and function.

Curricula

Parker has helped to develop all of the training materials that a congregation needs to teach, motivate, and equip members for ministry so that the body can build itself up in love. There are over 40 quarters (13 weeks per quarter) of training material available.

Assessments

Many members and church leaders would not know where to begin the task of helping disciples discover their spiritual gifts and the equipping training to turn those gifts into ministry that grows the church. We have just what you need.

Seminars

There are just too many resources to be presented here. The best place to start your journey is with a weekend introductory seminar.

Contact Forever Family Ministries

www.churchgrowthcrisis.com

Stephen Parker, MA, MSMFT

fam4evr@sbcglobal.net

405-443-4383

www.ingramcontent.com/pod-product-compliance
Lightning Source LLC
Chambersburg PA
CBHW060726110426
42738CB00056B/1716